There are not two voices I tru
of gender confusion than Dr.
Gender-Confident Kids, parents will learn the practical and biblical insights needed to guide their children through the doubt, confusion, and fear associated with a gender-confused culture, and affirm God's beautiful design for male and female. You will come away with a God-centered approach to this important issue and learn how to talk to your kids with compassion, hope, and truth—all guideposts for parents who want to approach gender dysphoria with confidence and grace. This book is a must-read for every parent of pre-teens and teens today!

Heidi St. John
Author, Speaker, and Host of the Heidi St. John Podcast

One of the most important questions any of us will ever face in life has to do with our identity. The Bible teaches us that God created each of us in his image as male or female. When we lose sight of that truth in the midst of chaotic and conflicting voices, heartache ensues. Kathy Koch and Jeff Myers offer practical strategies for helping our sons and daughters stay grounded in the truth of who God created them to be—and finding their identity in him.

Jim Daly
President, Focus on the Family

Raising Gender-Confident Kids is a timely, practical, and biblically-based book. While it is not alarmist, Myers and Koch write with a sense of urgency to counter many of the lies that are so prevalent in the world today. Whether your kids are struggling with their gender identity, or whether you want to get ahead of the game, I highly recommend this book.

Sean McDowell, Ph.D.
Professor of Apologetics at Talbot School of Theology, Author of *Chasing Love: Sex, Love and Relationships in a Confused Culture*, and Popular YouTuber

In a world filled with gender confusion, this book brings clarity, compassion, and truth for our children and grandchildren. Rooted in Scripture and packed with practical tools, it equips parents and leaders to guide kids toward confident, biblically grounded identity. From understanding core needs to confronting cultural lies, each chapter offers timely wisdom for raising the next generation in truth and love. A must-have resource for every faith-filled home.

Kirk Cameron
Actor, Author, Show Host

In *Raising Gender-Confident Kids*, Jeff and Kathy combine their expertise in powerfully important ways. For over two decades, I've used the 5 Core Needs and 8 Smarts that they use in the book in my home, schools, Bible studies, and ministries to help children and parents find clarity and confidence in Jesus and his design. I know these truths work! This book is practical, insightful, timely, clear, informative, and needed. It's a lifeline—and a must-read for every parent, grandparent, and faith leader navigating culture and guiding the next generation.

Suzanne Phillips
Founder of Beacon Parent, Host of The Informed Parent Podcast, Speaker, Parent Coach

Raising Gender-Confident Kids is a powerful blend of solid research and heartfelt wisdom. Dr. Jeff Myers and Dr. Kathy Koch offer not only deep insight into what helps kids thrive in a culture confused about gender, but also real-life stories and personal experiences that make the content practical and relatable. I applaud them for a job well done—this book is a valuable resource for parents, counselors, educators, and anyone who cares about raising gender-confident kids.

Mark Hancock
CEO, Trail Life USA

This is a terrific, concise guide filled with valuable insights and practical tips for raising kids with a biblically-based understanding of gender. In a culture that seems to grow in gender confusion daily, parents can't afford to not have clarity. *Raising Gender-Confident Kids* will help you gain that clarity so you can disciple your children with confidence on this pressing issue.

Natasha Crain
Speaker, Podcaster, and Author of Five Books

Raising Gender-Confident Kids is a powerful, faith-filled guide every Christian parent needs right now. In a world full of confusion, this book brings clarity, with deep biblical truth and real-life tools to help us raise children who are confident in who God created them to be. The authors don't just tell us why God's design matters—they show us how to raise secure, purpose-driven kids who can stand firm in truth while still loving others with the heart of Jesus. This isn't just about defending our kids from culture—it's about building their identity from the inside out, anchored in God's love and truth. I couldn't recommend it more.

Laine Lawson Craft
Bestselling Author of *The Parent's Battle Plan,* and Podcast Host

Our children today are under unique pressures growing up in the 21st century, and they need our help. Myers and Koch have given us as parents, teachers, extended family members, and professionals great direction. The final chapter on preparing both genders to stand for truth is worth the price of the book. I especially loved the straightforward answers to the 24 most asked questions at the end of the book. Kudos to Dr. Jeff Myers and Dr. Kathy Koch for standing in the gap with a flashlight to show us the way through the gender confusion surrounding our kids and helping us to help them embrace their God-given design.

Joe McIlhaney, MD
Founder and CEO, Medical Institute of Sexual Health

When two renown thought leaders on biblical worldview and child development collaborate on a work so important to these times, expectations are high. *Raising Gender-Confident Kids* hits the mark and clearly addresses the cultural moment and provides antidotes to the confusing messages confronting our children while providing clear calls to action. A must for every parent and grandparent's toolbox, I highly recommend this timely and important work. Our kids desperately need this message and these truths.

Patti Garibay
Founder and Executive Director Emeritus, American Heritage Girls

In *Raising Gender-Confident Kids*, Drs. Jeff Myers and Kathy Koch combine clinical expertise with a compassionate biblically-grounded approach to equip parents to nurture a deep sense of identity in their children. Their valuable insights offer practical ways to navigate today's cultural confusion, empowering families to engage in meaningful conversations that affirm God's design. This timely and insightful resource is a must-read for such a time as this for parents, educators, and anyone committed to instilling a healthy mindset in the next generation.

Tim Clinton, Ed.D., LPC, LMFT
President, American Association of Christian Counselors

Few Christian books today address gender identity without either compromising truth or lacking grace. Jeff Myers and Kathy Koch have written a compassionate and accessible guide for parents, drawing from child development theory, cultural analysis, and practical parenting strategies. In a world adrift in confusion, we rejoice that the redemptive work of Christ renews minds, reverses the curse of the Fall, and offers true confidence where there was confusion.

Christopher Yuan, D.Min.
Speaker, Author of *Holy Sexuality and the Gospel*, and Creator of The Holy Sexuality Project (holysexuality.com)

\
RAISING GENDER-CONFIDENT KIDS

KATHY KOCH, PHD
JEFF MYERS, PHD

HELPING KIDS EMBRACE THEIR GOD-GIVEN DESIGN

© 2025 Summit Ministries, Inc. and Celebrate Kids, Inc.

All rights reserved. No part of this publication may be reproduced, stored in a retrieval system, or transmitted in any form or by any means—for example, electronic, photocopy, recording—without the prior written permission of the publisher. The only exception is brief quotations in printed reviews.

Unless otherwise indicated, Scripture quotations are from the ESV® Bible (The Holy Bible, English Standard Version®), © 2001 by Crossway, a publishing ministry of Good News Publishers. Used by permission. All rights reserved. The ESV text may not be quoted in any publication made available to the public by a Creative Commons license. The ESV may not be translated in whole or in part into any other language.

Scripture quotations marked (TLB) are taken from The Living Bible, copyright © 1971 by Tyndale House Foundation. Used by permission of Tyndale House Publishers, Carol Stream, Illinois 60188. All rights reserved.

Published by Summit Ministries
PO Box 207
Manitou Springs, CO 80829

ISBN 978-1-9574-0651-0

Printed in the United States of America

genderconfidentkids.com

The content of this book is for religious, educational, and informational purposes only, and does not substitute for professional medical or counseling advice or consultations with healthcare professionals or counselors.

TABLE OF CONTENTS

PREFACE viii

CHAPTER 1 – How to Bring Confidence Out of Confusion—Four Keys Plus a Bonus **1**

CHAPTER 2 – Why Kids are Confused About Gender—Seven Causes **14**

CHAPTER 3 – Resolving "Identity Dysphoria" by Helping Kids Meet Five Core Needs **28**

CHAPTER 4 – How Scripture and a Biblical Worldview Strengthen Gender Confidence **45**

CHAPTER 5 – Four Biblical Truths that Refute Four Cultural Lies About Gender **59**

CHAPTER 6 – Guiding Boys to Become Confident Men by Using the Core Needs **74**

CHAPTER 7 – Guiding Girls to Become Confident Women by Using the Eight Smarts **89**

CHAPTER 8 – Guiding Boys and Girls, Men and Women to Harmonize—We Need Each Other **103**

CHAPTER 9 – Preparing Boys and Girls and You to Stand for Truth—Three Tested Strategies **111**

FAQs – Straightforward Answers to our 24 Most Frequently Asked Questions **127**

ACKNOWLEDGEMENTS 146
ABOUT THE AUTHORS 148
NOTES 152

PREFACE

Jeff began the video call with Kathy.

After chatting for a few minutes, he said, "I'd like to write a book speaking to the issue of gender confusion, but I remember you telling me you were working on something like that. I don't want to get in the way of one of your projects. Is that still something you're thinking about?"

"Yes! I'd love to write it, but it hasn't gotten off the ground yet."

"Maybe we could benefit from each other's expertise. Would you be open to working with me on a book Summit would publish?"

And just like that, *Raising Gender-Confident Kids* was born. What you hold in your hands isn't just for parents whose children are struggling with gender identity. We wrote to *prevent* the struggle. Every cultural confusion presents an opportunity. In this case, it's an opportunity for every parent to help every boy grow into a godly man and every girl into a godly woman. We pray it will be a blessing to you.

Preface

WHO WE ARE—AND HOW WE WROTE THIS

This book is a collaborative project. We (Jeff Myers and Kathy Koch) have spent decades serving students, parents, teachers, and leaders. Our two ministries—Summit Ministries and Celebrate Kids—work in tandem to equip the rising generation to embrace God's truth and reject cultural lies.

You'll hear both of our voices throughout the book. The chapters were drafted and refined together, combining our experience, teaching, and conversations. At the end of some chapters, you'll see individual "perspectives," personal reflections we hope encourage you.

We are united in our mission: to help you raise children who know who they are, trust who God is and who he made them to be, and live boldly in the truth.

HOW THIS BOOK WORKS

Each chapter focuses on a key question or challenge that families face as they nurture a child's identity. We explain what's happening culturally, explore what Scripture teaches, and offer practical strategies.

As you read, you'll see some pages marked with the tab, like the one on the right of this page. These mark **Conversation Starters**—questions, prompts, or scripts to help you in conversations with your kids and others. Talking with children about these topics is the most important thing you can do. We can't harvest what we don't plant. No two conversations are the same, and few turn out beautifully like they do in the movies. But, as Scripture says, gracious words are like gold apples on silver trays.[1]

They create long-lasting value even if they seem "blah" in the moment.

Finally, at the end of the book, you'll also find an FAQ section with our straightforward—but hopefully gracious—responses to the most common gender-related questions parents ask us.

GO DEEPER WITH ADDITIONAL RESOURCES

We created genderconfidentkids.com to accompany this book. There you'll find a full library of tools to help you go further:

- Audiobook and eBook access
- Downloadable tools and guides for every chapter
- All the conversation starters in one place
- Shareable content for friends, your church, or a small group
- Articles, podcasts, and teaching videos to extend your learning

Our prayer for this book is that it helps you build a way of life—one where God's truth is lived out in your family every day.

KEY TERMS

Before we delve deeper, we want you to understand how we define five key terms we use:

Gender. This book uses the term *gender*, rather than *sex*, to refer to male and female. This is for two reasons. First, while a person's identity includes both physiological and psychological traits, the term *gender* properly refers to male/female physiological traits. Gender is a design feature that is essential to what it means to be human, not just what it means to reproduce. Congruence between physiological and psychological traits is a central goal of gender confidence. We've included a little more detail about our reasoning in the endnote if you're curious.[2]

Second, we avoid the term *sex* to keep the focus on identity rather than sexual activity. Unfortunately, when people use the term *sex,* they don't mean sexual phenotype. They mean *having* sex. What we're talking about comes way before any such sexual choices are made. In our experience, for nearly all children, gender confusion is a question of "Who am I?" rather than "Who do I want to be intimate with?" We don't want anything to distract from this book's key question: *How can we help boys and girls be confident in how God designed them as male or female?*

Male/Female. Can you believe we have to define these? We'll use the terms *male* and *female* both theologically and physiologically. Theologically, male and female are the two kinds, the two *genera* of humanity, created to be distinctively different in a way that would harmonize for the good of the world. From a physiological perspective, there are 6,500 catalogued differences between male and female humans.[3] The most basic identifying feature of a male is that his gametes feature testes to produce sperm. A female's gametes feature ova to produce eggs. Despite the intentionally confusing rhetoric you've heard, it is physiologically impossible for a male to ever become a female, or vice versa.

Gender dysphoria. Fueled by activists and social media, many children are confused about their gender. The term *gender dysphoria* refers to "clinically significant distress" in someone who does not identify with their birth gender. If a person merely *dislikes* their gender without marked distress, or experiences normal adolescent discomfort with their body, that's not clinical dysphoria. True gender dysphoria is extraordinarily rare, but gender confusion is common. We'll address each of these with honesty and compassion.

Transgender. Transgender describes boys or men identifying and expressing themselves as girls or women and vice versa. This shift can appear in small steps, like changing clothing or hairstyles, or go as far as hormone therapies and surgeries.

Non-binary. Non-binary refers to people who reject male/female distinctions as relevant to their lives, or who believe that males and females are interchangeable.

YOU ARE NOT ALONE

We believe in you. We believe that God has called and equipped you to raise kids who are strong, wise, and confident in who he made them to be. And we believe that when you lean into this journey with compassion, hope, truth, and confidence, your children will thrive.

So, take a deep breath. Open your heart. Set aside any "woulda, shoulda, coulda." Be ready to speak the truth in love.

Let's raise gender-confident kids—together.

CHAPTER 1

HOW TO BRING CONFIDENCE OUT OF CONFUSION—FOUR KEYS PLUS A BONUS

"I have a question about my daughter." The mother's voice trembled, her tears interrupting every sentence. "She says . . . she says she was born in the wrong body. I try to talk with her, but she's shutting me out. What should I do?"

Every year, through our ministries—Summit Ministries and Celebrate Kids—we encounter thousands of students, teachers, parents, grandparents, counselors, and pastors who share similar stories. Recently, a single mom's face displayed a mixture of guilt and regret as she began talking. "I've been raising my son on my own, and things went great until he became a teenager. Now he seems so listless. How can I get him to do things that will build him into a man?" We're grateful to be trusted with such personal concerns and equally grateful that you're trusting us now. Thank you.

> We're going on a journey to discover how to raise gender-confident kids.

Together, we're going on a journey to discover how to raise gender-confident kids. The challenges are real, but it's important to know that God sees you and you're not alone. We've written this book to encourage you that you *can* raise children who are secure in how God made them. We want you to be confident in God's plan for boys and girls. We also have compassion for those who struggle, and a rock-solid belief that God's truth will give you the breakthroughs you need.

WHY WE NEED TO TALK ABOUT GENDER CONFUSION RIGHT NOW

Conversations about transgenderism, men in women's sports, and drag queen story hours have dominated the news over the last few years. And while the peak "woke era" may seem to have subsided, the cultural damage to America is extensive. Young adults ages 18 to 29 are now 1,600 times more likely than adults over 50 to say that their gender is different from what they were "assigned" at birth.[1]

Because we work with so many young people, we can say that this does *not* necessarily mean that a vast number of young people think they are male when they are female, or vice versa. Nor does it mean that they are engaged in homosexual relationships. In nearly every instance, it means, rather, that they don't see transgenderism as a stigma. They may even see it as cool or dismiss it as irrelevant to who they are.

How to Bring Confidence Out of Confusion—Four Keys Plus a Bonus

Every day, families feel they are at war. We spoke with one parent whose adopted child had begun "transitioning." The family essentially lost their parenting rights to the state, which is forcing the child into transgender treatments even though the family has strong evidence that serious psychiatric issues are going unaddressed in the process.

One middle school female went to an after-school "art class," which turned out to have been hosted by an outside organization pushing children into a transgender identity. The girl collapsed into depression, and while she is recovering, her family still deals with the fallout.

Even children who hadn't previously struggled with their gender identity are targeted, often by peers who feel "enlightened" by a TikTok video or have heard a classroom teacher pontificate about the "gender unicorn." One parent's middle school son was told by a peer, "If you haven't kissed a girl yet, that means you're gay."

And forget being able to call a counselor to help your child regain confidence in his or her gender. In 22 states, it is illegal for licensed therapists to counsel an alternative to transgender social and medical transitioning.

In many states, recent government policy changes seem to have paused the momentum of the transgender ideology's more tyrannical aspects, such as legal penalties for not using preferred pronouns, firings for "misgendering," and government forcing young women to compete in sports against biological males. But other states have doubled down, stripping away the rights of parents and schools. And the existing federal protections are essentially by executive order, meaning that a new president could quickly reverse them.

So, even if some aspects of the transgender agenda are fads, parents still face the tension: How do we help our girls grow into confident young women and our boys grow into confident young men? How do we persuade them to see that their gender is a valuable part of their God-given design?

How do we prepare them for a world that utterly rejects the values we are trying to impart to them?

Ultimately, our goals are to:

- **Explain** why gender confusion has spread and how it hurts kids.
- **Affirm** what God says and does in His special design for boys and girls, and how they can grow into godly men and women.
- **Equip** you to help your children trust God's best for their lives.
- **Guide** you through doubt, anger, or fear so you can boldly speak the truth in love.
- **Show** how to respond with godliness to the many ways that gender confusion shows up in kids.

> You can nurture kids who are strong in who they are—boys who are confident in their masculinity and girls who are confident in their femininity.

We believe that with practical and biblical insights, you can nurture kids who are strong in who they are—boys who are confident in their masculinity and girls who are confident in their femininity—each able to walk with heads held high.

In the coming chapters, we will seek to approach every topic with biblical instruction, practical strategies, and bold encouragement. First, though, we want to share the four postures at the heart of how we approach every issue facing young adults, not just gender confusion.

HOW TO LEAN INTO CULTURAL CONFUSION —FOUR POSTURES OF ENGAGEMENT

Picking up this book tells us a lot about you: you care deeply, want to learn, and are willing to be honest with your children. You believe they can embrace God's design for their lives. We'll broadly use terms like *kids* and *children* because gender confusion can surface in our children at any age—as toddlers, young children, teens, or young adults. If an idea applies to a specific age group, we'll say so.

We also hope grandparents, aunts, uncles, pastors, educators, counselors, and community leaders find value here. Although parents bear the primary responsibility for their children,[2] others have real influence, too. We honor these roles and invite you to join the conversation.

What posture should we have when we face cultural confusion? We think we should lean in, rather than lean away, even though our instinct tells it will be uncomfortable. Four postures guide us in engaging your heart and mind as well as your child's. These postures work together, fueling courage to model, teach, and defend God's design. They inspire kids to see things as they really are and act accordingly.

Posture #1: Compassion

Every parent wonders, "Am I doing enough?" Many carry guilt and sadness, while others feel fear, anger, and disappointment. These are heavy burdens God never intended us to carry alone. God wants us to develop hearts of compassion so we can guide our kids faithfully without compromising the truth.

When we meet struggling students, we tell them, "We hear you, we value the struggles you face, and we are confident that God is working in your life to align you with his truth." This breaks down barriers of defensiveness that keep kids stuck. God designed everything in his world to grow—including us!

Compassion is essential because gender struggles are complex. Some children feel genuine confusion. Others don't identify with cultural stereotypes about gender or have believed the lie that they've been born in the wrong body. Most are experiencing normal growth struggles and just need to know that God designed them the way he did on purpose. In all these situations, the Bible speaks. God is a compassionate God. He cares. And we have a steadfast hope that his caring nature will strengthen us and our families.

Posture #2: Hope

Compassion invites hope, which is the belief that a positive outcome is possible when we wait on God. Unlike naïve optimism, hope has a firm foundation.

Kathy keeps small pieces of gold twine in her home, purse, and briefcase as a powerful reminder of Isaiah 40:30–31, which promises renewed strength to those who hope in the Lord. She also wears a ring that resembles interwoven twine, a reminder of the Hebrew word *qavah*, meaning hope or wait, which refers to strands twisting together to form a durable cord.

Hope can be firmly woven into our lives because God is faithful.[3] And because God is faithful, we can assure our children, even when the conversations are challenging, that God is strengthening their spirits and weaving a beautiful tapestry in their lives.

Posture #3: Truth

With compassion and hope, we can help our children listen and learn. But we need to be prepared to give them more than our opinions. We need to orient them to the truth from God's Word.

Without a foundation in absolute truth, the rising generation is falling for propaganda. This includes an affinity for terrorist groups, supporting the confiscation of wealth, championing unrestricted abortion, and even normalizing lying when it protects their interests.

Today's young adult values are far from those held by previous generations. More importantly, these values are far removed from God's ways. We need God's truth to rise in their hearts and reveal the lies they're believing about many things, including gender.

We hope you agree that God's capital T *Truth* is the key, and we're eager to talk about God's amazing plan for gender. We think you'll be blown away by how good and wise God is. This book is accompanied by many other resources—including chapter downloads, articles, videos, and podcasts—that cover how God's wisdom helps boys aspire to be godly men and girls to aspire to be godly women. It can even inspire gender confidence in those who've become confused to the point that they see themselves as transitioning to the opposite gender.

One of our students at Summit Ministries, a biological female, had grown so confused about gender that she had begun taking masculinizing hormones. As she learned to embrace God's design for her life, she realized that she had been reacting to stereotypes of femininity that she didn't identify with. Her transition actions weren't making her happy, and it took a lot of courage to tell those who "encouraged" her that she wasn't going to continue transitioning but instead would seek satisfaction in the way God made her. We pray that this young woman continues to find good companions who help her see herself the way God sees her, rather than the way the culture wants her to be.

Compassion, hope, and truth change us! And they can change our kids!

Posture #4: Confidence

When compassion, hope, and truth are layered together, they build a strong foundation of confidence in our kids. The word *confidence* is made up of two ideas: *together* and *faith*. When we relate to our children's hearts and minds, they gradually learn to protect and nurture their own hearts and minds. This is a game-changer.

Confident people gather strength from trusted individuals to believe what is true and live in a new way. This is true for children, too. Being confident in their gender, children can develop a larger sense of how to be confident in God and His plan for their lives. Confidence is crucial!

Confidence in the right things is the foundation of many other essential building blocks, such as loving others, fixing your mistakes, not quitting when things get tough, facing fear, doing hard things, and connecting with those around you.

When we ask others what helps parents raise gender-confident kids, the conversation always comes back to our relationship with God. This includes knowing who we are in Christ, knowing he loves us no matter what, believing who God tells us we are, and seeking a deeper relationship with God.

Confidence in God is related to gender confidence as well as confidence in every other area of life. It's a process; don't lose hope if you're not there yet! We'll walk with you and share what we've learned that directly applies to raising children who love and honor God and one another.

Posture #4.1—Courage

Oh yes. There's one more. Let's call it a "bonus" that follows from the other four. Have you found that courage builds alongside confidence? That's true for us. Courage is confidence in action.

> **Courage is confidence in action.**

We don't want you to be brave so that you feel good about yourself. We want you to be brave so you can listen, guide, protect, lead, inspire, confront, walk with, correct, be present with, and love your children without condition.

To en*courage* someone means to give courage to them. We pray that this book encourages you to stay close to your children and far from the lies the culture tells about gender. We pray you'll be encouraged to hold forth the truth even when your children resist. Children can become defensive because they fear looking foolish or being wrong. It takes fortitude and resilience to break out of the mold that culture squeezes them into. We'll be praying for you and them.

FOUR ENEMIES THAT MAKE PEOPLE SHY AWAY FROM TOUGH ISSUES

People are not the enemy, even if they're confused or angry. Our enemies are **apathy**, **despair**, **lies**, and **doubt**. These forces are the opposites of compassion, hope, truth, and confidence. They deepen confusion about gender. The enemy of our souls[4] sows these traps to keep people from living as image-bearers[5] of God. He comes to steal identity, kill hope, and destroy the future.[6]

If children believe they're worthless, hopeless, or stuck, it's easy for them to entertain lies like, "There's no design or plan. I guess I can be whomever I want."

John 8:44 describes the devil as "the father of lies." He is the one we can be mad at. He tells parents and children they don't matter or that nothing matters (apathy). He tells them there's nothing to hope for or hope in (despair). He's persuasive, compelling, and manipulative because he has a strong agenda (lies). And he tickles the minds and hearts of children and parents with appealing messages contradicting what we know is best (doubt).

But you're not powerless. You can parent (and mentor) with clarity:

- **Fight apathy** by showing compassion.
- **Confront despair** with genuine hope.
- **Expose lies** by revealing the truth.
- **Overcome doubt** with confidence in God and his design.

You can parent for confidence—your and your kids'—because God is the author of truth, and he is on your side!

For now, we'll leave you with these insights. We know the battle is real. You know that—you're living in it. There are very real reasons children are deceived, confused, or certain of lies—like they can change their gender. We constantly ask parents to own their part of the problem, as appropriate, and give themselves massive amounts of grace, too. Changing children's beliefs and actions related to gender isn't easy. It is possible, though. We know that!

LET'S MOVE FROM GENDER CONFUSION TO GENDER CONFIDENCE!

We understand the seriousness of gender confusion; we've seen hearts break over it and families struggle through it. Yet we also believe there's real hope. You can come alongside your children with compassion, hope, truth, and confidence. You can help them recognize lies for what they are, see themselves as God's beloved, and grow into the men or women he designed them to be.

Wherever you are on this journey, remember:

- **You matter:** Your presence and influence are powerful in a child's life.
- **Your children matter:** God crafted them with a purpose, including the gender he gave them.
- **God matters most:** His unchanging nature offers the stability we all need.

Thank you for taking this step—your willingness to invest in these insights shows your commitment to your children's well-being. We pray you feel encouraged and better equipped to walk forward in compassion, hope, truth, and confidence.

Let's keep going together. Each chapter will explore how to guide children toward a biblical understanding of gender and identity, all while strengthening your own relationship with the One who created us for his glory. You're not alone, and you're exactly where you need to be—ready to learn, love, and lead.

We'll begin our exploration with a hard look at the culture to identify where gender confusion originates. We've highlighted seven causes that are tearing the rising generations apart and deepening the bitter divisions that fracture American society. Let's dig into those now.

DR. JEFF'S PERSPECTIVE
HOW THE INTERNET OVERWHELMS YOUNG ADULTS SEEKING THE TRUTH

It's hard to find the truth in a world overstuffed with information. Growing up, I loved asking about people's beliefs. I would point out the meeting houses of various religions and social groups and ask my mother, "What do they believe? How is that different from what we believe?"

Those are tough questions, but not impossible ones. A discerning person could examine a handful of competing claims and draw reasonable conclusions about their rightness or wrongness. Now, though, if you search *religion* on the internet, you'll get a billion results or more. As a child, I grappled with perhaps 20 belief systems, at most. Today's young adults grapple with millions.

To put this in perspective, imagine trying to find a genuine $100 bill in a stack of 20 counterfeits. The stack would be less than an inch high. But if you had a billion counterfeit bills, the stack would be 68 miles high. It would stretch from Earth into outer space. Trying to find the genuine bill would be nearly impossible.

The internet's inventors believed that if all the world's information could be gathered into one place, ignorance would be wiped out. Instead, people are more confused than ever. We don't have an *information* problem. We have a *formation* problem. Information is abundant; wisdom is scarce. That's why Scripture says, "Getting wisdom is the most important thing you can do!" (Proverbs 4:7, TLB).

> **We don't have an information problem. We have a formation problem."**

DR. KATHY'S PERSPECTIVE
HOW THE INTERNET OVERWHELMS PARENTS SEEKING THE TRUTH

Young adults aren't the only ones confused because of the internet. Many parents are, too. When my brother and I were young, we lived kitty-corner from our grandparents, my mom's parents. Our dad cut a hole in the fence, and we regularly walked back and forth between our homes and spent lots of time together. My mom conversed easily with her mom. We lived only four blocks from my dad's parents and just three blocks from my mom's sister, husband, and children. My mom and my Aunt Corky talked often about my brother, me, our four cousins, and what was happening in our schools, church, and community.

I walked to and from school with friends from our busy neighborhood. Moms waited for us to arrive home from school on one of several front porches where they compared notes on parenting and life in general. My mom and dad had a healthy community with family, neighbors, and friends from church.

How to Bring Confidence Out of Confusion—Four Keys Plus a Bonus

So many of today's parents don't have close family or friends to confide in, or they choose not to be vulnerable with them. Instead, many moms post their parenting questions on social media. Some are trusting input about feeding children, bedtime, school choice decisions, obedience, punishments, and so much more to people they barely know.

Between social media posts, websites, search engines, apps, podcasts, and millions of books available online, parents have easy and quick access to information, and much of it's free. I'm afraid, however, that they're lacking wisdom. They have answers to this and that, but no cohesive parenting style. Most haven't considered the values that should drive their parenting decisions. The ease of easy answers appears to make parenting philosophies unnecessary. Therefore, they flit from gentle parenting to authoritarian parenting to panda parenting to permissive parenting. Now they're confused, and so are their children. Confusion is *never* good.

Just because something is readily available doesn't mean we need to use it.

Want help navigating the internet with wisdom? Download the Chapter One resource, "Sorting Truth from Noise," at genderconfidentkids.com.

CHAPTER 2

WHY KIDS ARE CONFUSED ABOUT GENDER—SEVEN CAUSES

If you know someone who is gender confused, we're guessing that you've racked your brain trying to figure out how it happened. It's maddening to contemplate the powerful forces working to destroy our children.

Many children are confused and angry as well. Kathy visited with an older teen who admitted to feeling angry with herself when she realized she had been tricked into believing things Scripture did not support. More than once, she mumbled, "How could I have been so stupid for so long?" Kathy calmly repeated, "You haven't been stupid. You were deceived." At last, the young woman's countenance changed as she began to process this truth.

We're not suggesting that moving from "feeling stupid" to "being deceived" made everything okay. But for that young woman, it changed her trajectory; now she's headed into a different—and far better—orbit. She recognized she was still responsible for her beliefs but found freedom from the self-condemnation that makes change difficult. She longed for a different future. She had begun to "hunger and thirst for righteousness" (Matthew 5:6).

Just as this young woman was helped by understanding the falsehoods she had believed, we want you to understand what can cause children's misunderstandings about gender. In this chapter, we'll share the influences that have caused gender confusion and gender dysphoria to settle, covertly, into the hearts of a whole generation.

Beliefs cause behavior. If you want behavior change, you must replace false beliefs with true ones. In this chapter, we'll identify who and what influences the rising generation's false beliefs about gender. Then, in other chapters, we'll get practical, showing how to replace untrue beliefs with true ones based on God's Word.

Cause #1: Sin and Ignorance of God's Best

Let's agree that sin and ignorance about God's principles and standards cause some of the chaos we find ourselves navigating. We need to be prepared to call sin, *sin*, with a goal of leaving the sin behind and taking responsibility for what happens next.

Yet much of our culture's gender confusion affects believers because they haven't been effectively discipled in understanding what's right and wrong according to God's Word. Many look to Scripture for comfort, but we

> **Believers haven't been effectively discipled in understanding what's right and wrong according to God's Word.**

don't contemplate how it speaks to everything, everywhere, all the time. We pray when we're in trouble, but don't rely on the Holy Spirit for peace, self-control, and conviction. We want God to give us good things, but we ignore the boundaries he has established for our benefit and feel indifferent to how our sin grieves him. We are vulnerable when attempting to live out this skin-deep faith.

Can you imagine with us what could happen if God's power transformed the minds of the rising generation?[1]

Dare we hope for a generation that becomes strong by "putting on the whole armor of God"?[2]

We see signs of hope. Barna Group reported encouraging news in January 2025.[3] Over three in four US teens (77%) say they are at least somewhat motivated to continue learning about Jesus throughout the rest of their lives. Fewer than one in five are unmotivated. Interest in Jesus makes a tremendous difference, but information alone isn't sufficient. True and lasting change happens when God's Word transforms our hearts, uproots false beliefs, and replaces lies with the truth.[4] God's Word gives us a standard by which to live, releasing us to change from the inside out.

Let's back up, though. The starting point is to confess with our mouths that Jesus is Lord and believe in our hearts that God has raised him from the dead.[5] We must accept that Scripture's teaching is true and intentionally model and talk about why that is so. It's this all-of-life commitment that we want our children to embrace.

We shouldn't be surprised that people who don't know God and his ways will have an "anything goes" mentality toward much of life, including gender. They may have heard or read that God created us "male and female" (Genesis 1:27), but that doesn't mean they believe it is relevant to how they live.

These are different days. We both remember a time in America when people generally agreed about right and wrong. Whether people attended church or not, most agreed that stealing was wrong and respecting others was right. They intuitively recognized that boys are boys and girls are girls. Moral relativism changed all that, and gender confusion thrives on the false notion that we each decide our own truth.

THINK ABOUT IT

How are you reacting to the role ignorance and sin play in gender confusion? How does this make you feel? Would children agree? And how do you think it makes them feel? How can this influence how you share truth with children and express your compassion and hope? How does it affect the way you help children gain confidence about God and his plans for their lives? How might your thoughts and feelings result in additional action? Will they?

Cause #2: The Rapid Rise of Radical Gender Ideology

For millennia, it was assumed that every person is born either male or female. It's a biological reality: humans are sexually dimorphic. As we noted in the preface, there are 6,500 biological differences between males and females.[6] But as twentieth century academic thinking took a postmodern turn, radical scholars began to teach that reality isn't something "out there" for which we must account. Rather, it is something we "construct" for ourselves. In this mindset, *all* categories must be called into question, even male and female.

Transgenderism became a wedge hammered between us and reality. After decades of taking root in the musty halls of academia, transgenderism exploded across America. For some, it was little more than a way to relieve the normal body discomfort that comes with puberty. For others, though, it was seen as a bulwark from which the "patriarchal" structure of society could be dismantled.

Some of the fastest growth in those identifying as gender dysphoric has been among teen girls. In 2018, Lisa Littman, a public health researcher, labeled it "rapid onset gender dysphoria." She found that social media immersion explained two-thirds of transgender identification in young girls.[7] And there is no question that the rise of transgender and nonbinary thinking is a social media phenomenon. At its height, on the popular social media platform TikTok, *#trans* logged 50.2 billion views.

> The latest research indicates that medical transition doesn't help the situation and frequently worsens it.

Lost in all the hoopla is that about five to ten out of every hundred thousand children, primarily boys, suffer from severe discomfort in their bodies, which is what led to mental health professionals developing the diagnosis of gender dysphoria in the first place.[8] The psychological anguish they feel is painful, and our hearts go out to them. Most often, treatment for the underlying psychological issues, such as anxiety, depression, or abuse, causes these symptoms to ease. However, the latest research indicates that medical transition doesn't help the situation and frequently worsens it.

THINK ABOUT IT

How did you react when reading about how unbiblical gender ideologies became mainstream? How do you think knowing this might make children feel? How can we help our children understand that just because something gets talked about a lot doesn't make it true? What are some things that make it hard to express compassion and hope to those who are struggling? How might your thoughts and feelings result in additional action? Will they?

Cause #3: A Twisted Approach to Mental Health Struggles

Current research supports what we've seen and believed: many children who are insecure in their gender have diagnosed or undiagnosed mental health conditions. These can include depression, stress, anxiety, and despair. A 2020 article by authors sympathetic to gender transition treatment reviewed 37 studies and found that 40–45 percent of children experiencing gender dysphoria also suffer from significant additional mental health issues.[9] We suspect the real figure to be much higher. Jeff has worked with many transgender-identifying young people over the years and has yet to meet one who did not also express multiple mental health concerns. Children unhappy with their gender are often lonely or overwhelmed and feel insignificant, confused, and dissatisfied with their lives.

> We take mental health struggles seriously. We feel deep compassion for those who struggle and want them to improve.

They want to believe that changing their gender will bring relief. To them, it seems like a simple and obvious solution. But it's not.

In too many places, and certainly in public schools controlled by people who embrace transgender ideology, diverse expressions of gender are something to be proud of. When students announce they want to change their gender, they receive enthusiastic affirmation. Sadly, the feeling of acceptance is short-lived, and it often aggravates underlying mental health issues.

We also want to add that many children who may be depressed, stressed, lonely, or hopeless are not and will not question their gender. These struggles are not a guarantee of confusion, but the connection is common enough that we need to point it out.

As professionals who work closely with young adults and parents of children of all ages, we take mental health struggles seriously. We feel deep compassion for those who struggle and want them to improve. We want their parents to be strong, too.

THINK ABOUT IT

Have you seen a relationship between mental health struggles and transgenderism? Have your children noticed? Why do you think so many struggling people automatically assume that the struggles they face can be solved by announcing a transgender or nonbinary identity? How can you talk about this with children so they hear the truth and experience compassion and hope? How might your thoughts and feelings result in additional action? Will they?

Cause #4: The Manipulation of Language

Behind the novelty of transgenderism is a radical ideology held by people who want to influence and control language because they know words teach and create. Words make the world, transgender activists believe, and they thrive on creating terms that force people to affirm the transgender belief system. Men who see themselves as women are called "trans women." Women who see themselves as men are "trans men." Children are told that their gender is "assigned at birth" and that their doctor may have been mistaken.[10] Preferred pronouns have been mandated in schools and many companies, and those who "misgender" others can lose their jobs, their reputations, and in some states, have their children taken away from them. Activists promoting these changes scorn concerns about free speech and conscience. They believe that if they write the dictionary, they can eventually make words only mean what they want them to mean. Opposition will be impossible because there will be no vocabulary with which to express it.

Another example of gender ideology's manipulation of language is the phrase "gender-affirming care" (GAC). That sounds so nice and positive, right? Of course, we want to affirm our children's gender. But that's not what this phrase means to those who support transgenderism. It's the exact opposite. They mean we should affirm the *new* gender someone wants. Therefore, GAC recommends a path of social transitioning that leads inevitably to medical transitioning. We feel so strongly about the danger of this phrase that when we use it, we call it "so-called gender-affirming care."

THINK ABOUT IT

We must define our words and use them carefully and accurately. We should also ask others what they mean by the words they use. How do you think children feel about this issue? Ask them if they can share times when words were used against them. How can understanding the language issue influence how you share truth with children and express your compassion and hope? How might your thoughts and feelings result in action? Will they?

Cause #5: The Ideological Capture of Public Schools

Transgender ideology is prevalent in public schools. An analysis of Centers for Disease Control data shows that fully *half* of the public schools in America actively encourage teachers to implement "inclusive" practices such as preferred pronouns and to make accommodations based on transgender and nonbinary identity.[11] Staff regularly teach that there are more than two genders and that every child can choose any identity they like. Characters in books such as *When Aiden Became a Brother*, *My Rainbow*, and *Sparkle Boy* tell children that it is easy and fun to change genders, it brings joy, and it will make them popular.[12]

In the schools that embrace transgender ideology, school district leaders *force* teachers to engage in gender ideology propaganda against their will. Most teachers oppose this. Two-thirds of elementary teachers say that children shouldn't learn about gender identity at school. Four in ten K–12 teachers say that gender ideology makes it harder to do their jobs. Just four percent say such debates have a positive impact.[13]

Parents are increasingly uncomfortable with what is happening in schools, and that's good. Up to 80 percent of parents don't want schools trying to "help" children change their gender identity.[14] More and more brave teachers, professors, and coaches are taking a stand. The girls' basketball coach at one school Summit Ministries has worked with forfeited a game rather than force his players to compete against a team with a male player. The state athletic association severely punished his school. After much prayer and discussion, the school took the issue to the courts. This has given other schools the courage to take a stand.

One college athlete described her experience of having to share a dressing room with a biological male who subsequently won the top spot in a national tournament. When asked about this travesty, she said, "I wondered two things: 'Why won't the athletic association protect female athletes?' and *'Where are the dads?'*" That last question haunts us. Until more parents stand up and say, "Enough is enough," America's young people are going to be cast into confusion that risks long-lasting trauma.

THINK ABOUT IT

Let's look for opportunities to talk with friends and family about how schools have influenced children's thinking. Practice explaining your perspective so you're confident and able to influence others. How do you think the school's beliefs make children feel? How can you share truth with children and express your compassion and hope? How might your thoughts and feelings result in action? Will they?

Cause #6: Media Bias, the Internet, and Platforming of Lies

Public schools are not the only institutions that choose to align with an inaccurate and manipulative ideology surrounding gender. Far too many

Why Kids are Confused About Gender—Seven Causes

media outlets intentionally ignore viewpoints that challenge the gender ideology narrative. Testimonies of detransitioners—those who changed their gender and then realized it was wrong—are almost entirely excluded from coverage in the legacy media.[15] Also excluded is the research showing that transgender medical and surgical intervention does not diminish suicidality.[16]

When we had questions growing up, we asked an adult. Today, children ask Google. And what do they find? Just now, we typed *transgender* into the Google search engine. The top results all strongly promote transgenderism, proclaiming that they're providing "facts" about the issue and showing transgender-identifying people how to get medical treatment and legally separate from their parents. You'll have to go several pages deep to find *any* information that challenges the transgender narrative. And if Google is biased this way, Instagram and TikTok are far worse.

> **Far too many media outlets intentionally ignore viewpoints that challenge the gender ideology narrative.**

Many parents are caught off guard by this. They're shocked when their children believe the false and manipulative ideas they've "researched" on the internet. Often, children take advantage of this power shift to disrespect their parents, win arguments with them, and make them feel insecure and guilty. If this has happened to you, we are so sorry. We hope you haven't carried guilt and shame. Many children have been coached—consciously and unconsciously—in school and by their peers to behave this way.

Do not judge the entirety of your parenting based on a lost argument about gender or even that you argued at all. These are challenging times, and we understand. We sincerely want our words to release you from guilt and shame and increase your peace and confidence. We will continue to get very practical so you can overcome past negative experiences and walk confidently in truth.

THINK ABOUT IT

Plan to talk with children about what you notice in the media, on the web, and from social media and apps. Ask where they turn when they have questions about gender, what they notice, and how they feel about it. Help them evaluate why they make their choices and whether they're wise choices. How do you think it would make children feel if they understood how the gender issue is lied about? How can the media bias influence how you share truth with children and express your compassion and hope? How might your thoughts and feelings result in action? Will they?

Cause #7: Medical Professionals Blinded to the Truth

Radical transgender ideology works hand in hand with a greedy medical industry manipulating teens, young adults, and parents for power and profit.[17] It's sickening to think that medical professionals, whom most people instinctively trust, would seek to make money off gender-insecure people. But it's happening. Puberty-blocking treatments cost up to $35,000 a year, and cross-sex hormones, which are less expensive to produce, can yield enormous profits.[18] Add to this the burgeoning practice of surgically removing healthy breasts and genitals, and you've got a highly lucrative business because lifelong medical treatment will be necessary.

All this medical intervention is based on a lie. Biological sex can't be changed. It's a permanent and good part of God's intentional plan for us. Puberty blockers, cross-sex hormones, and surgery gravely harm children pursuing a physical impossibility. More and more people are seeing it as a child abuse scandal in which underlying mental health challenges are left unaddressed in the rush to medically treat symptoms of gender dysphoria rather than its causes. And because the physical changes don't make a girl a boy or a boy a girl, and there are medical and social complications, mental health struggles become more difficult.

Why Kids are Confused About Gender—Seven Causes

We're encouraged that people are beginning to see that we can't trust what has been touted as "science." In the summer of 2024, Hilary Cass, a respected British medical doctor and former president of the Royal College of Paediatrics and Child Health in England, released a 388-page report that led to significant changes in her nation's treatment of gender dysphoria. Drawing on 200 different sources, Cass revealed the poor quality of research about transgender treatments and concluded that the rationale for puberty blockers is unclear, and that long-term evidence of cross-sex hormone treatment effectiveness is nonexistent. She also found there were no clear standards of screening for childhood trauma or mental health comorbidities such as anxiety, depression, and autism. She concluded that the field of transgender medicine for minors is a mess.[19]

The World Professional Association for Transgender Health (WPATH) rejected the Cass report in the strongest terms because it went against what they believe and recommend. This powerful organization, wholly given over to transgender ideology, developed the standards of care by which US doctors are supposed to treat gender confusion. We're grateful for the investigative journalists who have uncovered the way WPATH officials regularly worked to squelch the results of studies that didn't affirm their approach. WPATH's credibility is now in shambles as the political interests behind its manipulation have been unmasked. We've all been lied to!

We began writing this book shortly after President Trump was inaugurated on January 20, 2025. As of this writing, he has already introduced four executive orders that directly affect gender, including one that declares there are only two genders—male and female.[20] Naturally, some people are angry, but most are grateful. Many school boards, corporations, and associations changed their policies in response. For example, on February 6, 2025, the National Collegiate Athletic Association (NCAA) announced that women's sports will be limited to student-athletes assigned female at birth.[21] As of this writing, 27 states have enacted laws restricting the experimental use of medical technology to treat transgenderism in minors.[22] The federal government has also recently removed funding for such treatment. We expect other announcements to follow. But we also expect pushback from states controlled by the progressive left (such as Colorado, where Summit Ministries is headquartered). Now is not the time to let down our guard.

THINK ABOUT IT

Are you aware of parents or children hurt by the philosophies and actions of medical professionals? Why might it be good to let children know about lies and manipulation? How do you expect them to feel? How can understanding this influence the way you share truth with children and express your compassion and hope? How might your thoughts and feelings result in action? Will they?

The #1 Reason These Causes of Gender Confusion Prevail

All of these attacks—spiritual, ideological, mental, educational, and medical—succeed with children because they promise a shortcut to answering life's "Who am I?" question. If we want our children to be gender confident, we must be intentional in nurturing their process of identity formation. Without a strong identity, they'll flounder and be at the mercy of the voices around them. For example:

- If they answer, "Who am I?" with "I am popular," they'll have to make choices to keep themselves popular. But what happens if people stop paying attention to them? You'd be surprised at how many children "come out" as transgender after being heavily influenced by their desire for attention. They know they'll get it.
- If physical attractiveness is their everything, they'll panic when someone better-looking walks into the room, they don't like

Why Kids are Confused About Gender—Seven Causes

their hair that day, or they wear something that others tease them about. What if an influential teacher or peer convinces them that they're in the wrong body and that a change of gender would make them more attractive?

> **If we want our children to be gender confident, we must be intentional in nurturing their process of identity formation.**

- If performing well is most important, they could learn to cheat or not take risks because it's easy to succeed or to fake success. If doing well is their goal, it will be easier for people to convince children to change their gender because they are more likely to succeed.

How do children arrive at healthy answers to the "Who am I?" question? One of the main ways is by identifying and nurturing five core needs every child has. You have a lot of influence here!

In the next chapter, we'll examine each of the needs—why each is important, what makes each healthy, actions you can take to be the influence you want to be, and how God is the best at meeting these needs.

> You can grow in your ability and confidence in identifying bad ideas before they influence your family. Download the Chapter Two resource, "Fighting the Lies That Shape Our Culture," at genderconfidentkids.com.

CHAPTER 3

RESOLVING "IDENTITY DYSPHORIA" BY HELPING KIDS MEET FIVE CORE NEEDS

We've talked with parents who feel hopeless because the tidal wave of gender ideology has crashed into their homes. Reading about the roots of gender confusion in the last chapter may have discouraged you. We get it. But the good news is that you can build a strong foundation of gender confidence—and overall confidence—by focusing on five core needs that every child has, which are met fully through God.[1]

MEETING FIVE CORE NEEDS LEADS TO HEALTH AND FLOURISHING

As Kathy has taught and written about for years, God creates each of us with five core needs. When we trust God to meet these needs, we experience health and flourishing. We'll now be resilient against manipulation and lies. On the other hand, when we try to meet these needs in anyone or anything but God, we'll be vulnerable to wherever cultural winds blow.

In our experience, mental health challenges and unwise choices can be traced back to unmet needs. This is true for adults as well as children. We've worked with many who have turned to drugs, alcohol, promiscuity, hate, perfectionism, jealousy, adrenaline rushes, and busyness, all in attempts to meet their core needs on their own.

In this book, we've talked about gender dysphoria, clinically significant distress about gender. In our experience, gender dysphoria stems from a generalized "identity dysphoria" that leads to depression, anxiety, suicidal ideation, apathy, abuse, and anger.

The earlier we notice and work to correct faulty thinking about core needs, the better our chance that "small" doubts, dissatisfactions, and fears don't snowball into bigger issues, like gender confusion. And the clearer we are about having core needs met through God, the more our children will be able to discern the difference between needs and their wants—instant happiness, freedom from pain, acceptance—that make them vulnerable to wrong ideas about gender.

> **When you equip children to discover and believe that God abundantly meets their needs, the more they can enjoy identity confidence.**

Here are the five core needs and their defining questions. The order is significant, as we'll demonstrate. When you equip children to discover and believe that God abundantly meets their needs, the more they can enjoy identity confidence!

- Security: Who can I trust?
- Identity: Who am I?
- Belonging: Who wants me?
- Purpose: Why am I alive?
- Competence: What do I do well?

Let's look at each of these, beginning with the foundation—security—to discern why each is important, what actions we can take, and how to rely on God to meet them.

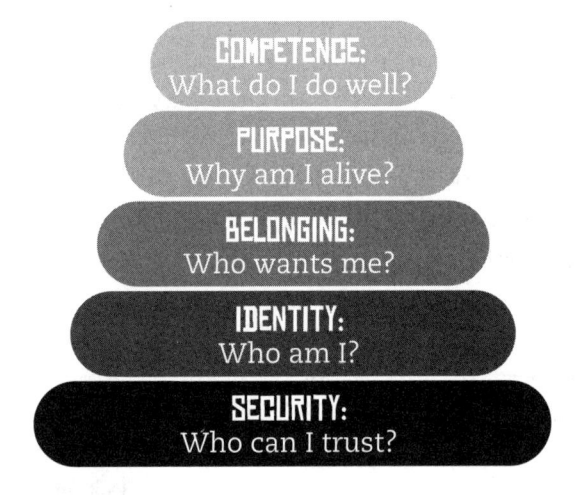

COMPETENCE: What do I do well?

PURPOSE: Why am I alive?

BELONGING: Who wants me?

IDENTITY: Who am I?

SECURITY: Who can I trust?

Core Need #1: Security—Who Can I Trust?

Children need security to be emotionally, socially, and physically safe and free from danger, fear, and anxiety. Security is healthiest when children trust Christ for their salvation, depend on and follow God's ways, and rely on him and trustworthy, dependable people. Trusting *in* God leads to being trustworthy *before* God and doing the right thing even when no one is watching. It leads to discernment.

Resolving "Identity Dysphoria" by Helping Kids Meet Five Core Needs

Sadly, those who send confusing messages to children about gender have learned to present themselves as trustworthy. They're just presenting the "facts," they say. They promise to be present for desperate children and solve their problems for them. When it comes to gender confusion, they'll answer all their questions about transitioning their gender to make the journey "easy."

Children must have their need for security met. Otherwise, when people disappoint or manipulate them, they may cope by putting their security in what they can do rather than who they are as beloved children of God. It might be class rank, how many *likes* an Instagram reel gets, making the starting basketball roster, or anesthetizing themselves in a social media world that makes them feel like the center of reality. But this never lasts. They'll always need "one more thing," whether admiration, money, position, grades, or comfort.

When Kathy teaches about core needs, she asks if people believe there's an identity crisis in our culture. Heads nod. She then points out the order of the needs and boldly instructs, "We have an identity crisis in our culture because we have a security crisis. If children have no one to trust, they can't know who they are." You can hear a pin drop after she says this. Is this how you're reacting?

Be trustworthy so children can count on you to be an excellent source of security. Point them to God as their ultimate security.

Take action: Meeting the core need for security means helping children be free *from* caring about the things that consume the time and attention of most people, so they can be free *to* discover their gifts and be a blessing. Security builds through everyday conversations:

- **When they've done something frustrating:** "I'm frustrated right now, but I'm never going to give up on you and I don't want you to ever give up on knowing that your security comes from God."

- **When they've made a good decision:** "One of the most important things in life is doing what you say you're going to do. In that situation you were trustworthy and I'm proud of you."
- **When they face a tough decision:** "Let's pray together for wisdom because it isn't just who and what you say 'No' to, it's who and what you say 'Yes' to. I want you to feel protected to say 'Yes' to the right things even when it's hard."
- **When they're unhappy with your decision:** "It seems like you feel mad at me right now. That's okay. My goal is to discern and do what God wants, even when it doesn't make you happy."
- **When they ask a tough question:** "That's a hard question. I feel like I should know the answer, but I don't. Can I take some time to think and pray about it?"
- **When they have been offended:** "I sense that your feelings have really been hurt by someone. You have to decide whether to forgive them and move on. Staying mad hurts you more than it hurts the other person."

Conversations like these help children discern who to trust, who is on their side, who has not been a good friend, and how to distance themselves from being hurt or influenced to do what is wrong. The wrong question is, "What can I trust?" So, if you notice them trusting in things, talk about it. People can't be healthy if they believe they are what they possess.

> Wait expectantly for God. Celebrate spiritual growth. Worship with honesty. Ask for forgiveness. Be reliable. Elevate principles worth believing in.

God answers the security question best. "Who can I trust?" I can trust God who created me because he had so much love to share, Jesus who took my sin upon himself so I would be saved and restored to right standing, and the Holy Spirit who guides, comforts, teaches, and convicts. Everyone is someone Jesus died for, created in God's image, and deeply loved.[2] Believers are also dead to sin and alive to Christ, set free, transformed, and more than conquerors.[3]

Children will want the Triune God to meet their need for security when they see that you depend on God in all you do. Pray passionately with them and for them. Read God's Word in times of need and for encouragement, not just at church. Wait expectantly for God's answers. Celebrate spiritual growth. Worship with honesty. Ask for forgiveness. Be reliable. Elevate principles worth believing in, even when people around us fail, as they undoubtedly will.

Core Need #2: Identity—Who Am I?

Children want to be known. They need to be known because God created them that way. He knows every hair on their heads! Identity is healthiest when children know they are intentionally and uniquely designed by a loving God. This makes it possible for them to have an accurate, current, and complete view of who they are.

Children gravitate to people who know them. Children fall for transgender ideology—and other ideologies—because it gives them an identity. They hear, "Your parents may not understand you, but we do. We know what it's like to feel you were born in the wrong body. We support you."

Children with fragile identities are vulnerable to strangers offering understanding and support. But you can inoculate your child against falsehood by building a foundation of emotional support in everyday situations, whether you're talking about gender or anything else. The message is: "I understand. How can I support you?" If your son tells you he's nervous about a test, say, "I get it. But, remember, you've been doing better. I'm for you. How can I support you?" On the morning of the test, encourage him and pray for him out loud. At the end of the day, say, "I hope you feel good about today's test." Stay present in case he wants to give you details.

If your daughter talks about a friend she's concerned about, acknowledge her compassion and say, "I get it. I'm glad you're compassionate and yet it's tough when you care about someone, and things aren't going well. I'm here anytime if I can help." You can say, "I remember having a situation like that and I'd be happy to share how I handled it. Would that be helpful?" Then ask about this friend and their relationship a day or two later. Set an alarm on your phone to remind you if you need to. This demonstrates that your daughter is a high priority.

THREE CHARACTERISTICS OF HEALTHY IDENTITIES

A healthy identity is **accurate**. Because our confidence is in God, it's okay to admit that we have challenges and strengths in answering the "Who am I?" question. If you hear children say something about themselves that isn't true, you must correct them, whether their comment is an unwarranted boast or self-criticism. Identity controls behavior; who they think they are is who they will be. They'll assume you agree unless you bring it up. Not bringing it up can harm their behavior and damage your relationship. If you can, determine the source of the lie so you can direct children to distance themselves from that person or source.

A strong identity is also **current**. It doesn't live in the past or the future. Many people make decisions out of fear of repeating past mistakes or a desire to reclaim the glory of a past triumph. The question should be "Who *am* I?" not "Who *was* I?" Be careful of talking too much about what happened in the past, who they used to hang out with, who you disapproved of, or a decision they now regret. Your motivation is to encourage your child's progress and not simply remind them of past unwise choices.

Resolving "Identity Dysphoria" by Helping Kids Meet Five Core Needs

Also, don't let them live too much in the "Who *could* I be?" world. One of Jeff's students said, "I've spent so much time planning for what's next that I forget to be present in the now." It's a powerful admission. Do you remember much about your senior year in high school? You may not because you were so focused on what you hoped would happen after graduation. Thinking of the future is essential to our need for purpose, but what makes the future bright is how we make the most of the present moment. We tell young people that their dreams for tomorrow start now.

> They are so much more than a boy or a girl. They're a beloved child of God, the Creator of the universe, and the One who saves them!

Healthy identities are also **complete**. We suspect that a reason gender confusion has become all-consuming to some children is that they have forgotten the rest of who they are. They are so much more than a boy or a girl. They're a beloved child of the God who is the Creator of the universe and the One who saves them! In your prayer and conversation, remind them—and yourself—of what it means to be made in God's image. When stressed, remember: "I am God's child!" When you're feeling "blah," remember: "I am God's child!"

Be involved so children can count on you to be an excellent source of identity. Point them to God as the author of their identity.

Take action: Affirm children's strengths by paying attention to what they do well that returns energy to them and makes them feel more alive. Avoid pride; encourage confidence. Talk about challenges positively so they will work to improve them and accept those that can't be changed. Here are some conversation reminders:

- **In a tough situation:** "Wow, this seems really uncomfortable. Let's just pause for a moment and take a breath. 'God, would you be with us in this moment as we figure out what to do?'"

- **When their attitude turns sour:** "We can't control everything around us, but we can control our attitude. Let's step back for a minute and reset."
- **When they're overly self-critical:** "I hear that you're discouraged. But when you say, 'I always' or 'I never,' those aren't true statements. You've got what it takes to move forward, even if just an inch."
- **When they're overly sensitive to failure:** "Your worst moments don't define you. Neither do your best moments. You're brave. You're learning to understand yourself. You're growing. You're going to be okay."

The wrong questions are "Who was I?" and "Who could I be?" So, stay focused on the present and teach them how today's beliefs, attitudes, and decisions affect their future.

God answers the identity question best. "Who am I?" I am who God says I am. I believe Scripture, so I believe he is a good Creator. Believers are forgiven, God's workmanship, complete in Christ, free from condemnation, and have the righteousness of God through Christ and peace beyond understanding.[4]

Children will want the Triune God to meet their need for identity when they see that you depend on all of God. Demonstrate that God is a God of new beginnings and second chances. He totally forgives us and chooses to forget we ever sinned. Model that you are free in Christ, a new creation, that Jesus is not just your Savior but your Lord, and that the Holy Spirit is your guide, teacher, and constant companion. Our identity is also positively affected when we pray, study the Word, worship, reflect, confess, and forgive.

Resolving "Identity Dysphoria" by Helping Kids Meet Five Core Needs

Core Need #3: Belonging—Who Wants Me?

Children need belonging because God created us to have a relationship with him and with people. Healthy belonging results from a growing relationship with God and strong relationships with trustworthy people, especially the family. Being accepted and connecting well with others bolsters children's security, informs their identity, readies them to live on purpose, and provides reasons to be competent.

Be available so children can count on you to be an excellent source of belonging.

Take action: Work to establish healthy security and a complete and positive identity so relationships come more easily and children choose not to isolate. For example:

- **In a new situation:** "I'm going to be praying that God will help you be respectful, attentive, cooperative, caring, kind, and patient today."
- **When they're around others:** "People are drawn to those who enter a room with 'There you are!' enthusiasm rather than a 'Here I am!' posture. It also makes you less nervous."
- **When social media dominates their actions:** "I'm learning that when we're on our phone, it makes others feel taken for granted. I want to encourage you to put your phone down and see those around you as God sees them."
- **When they need assurance:** "It's so easy to get distracted and I know I'm guilty of it, too. I love you and will always love you and am praying that you'll feel settled and caring toward others."

The wrong question is, "Who needs me?" Instead, focus on the value of being wanted and the qualities that make them pleasant to be around.

God answers the belonging question best. "Who wants me?" God wants me for who I am and not because of what I do. Believers are accepted in Christ, never forsaken, comforted, Christ's friend, adopted, called by name, and more.[5]

Children will want the Triune God to meet their need for belonging if they see that you depend on all of God. Talk about how quiet time with God, without an agenda, meets our need for belonging to God. You can make a case for the relevance of church involvement, communion, fellowship, serving, giving, worship, the Word, and prayer.

Core Need #4: Purpose—Why Am I Alive?

Purpose means what we're aiming for. Children need purpose to live and love well. Purpose is healthiest when children have hope that they can discover and use their God-given skills and passions to glorify him and positively influence the world. Gender-confident kids grow aware of why they're alive and why their strengths and skills matter. Purpose motivates children to discover and believe in their competence.

> Purpose is healthiest when children have hope that they can discover and use their God-given skills and passions to glorify him.

Be hopeful so children can count on you to be an excellent source of purpose. Point them to God as their ultimate purpose.

Take action: Bolster belonging so children have people to love and serve.

- **When they are uncertain:** "Most of the great heroes in the Bible felt afraid about what God wanted them to do. 'Do not be afraid' is the most repeated command in the Bible. One thing I know is that God made you on purpose. I am trusting that he has already given you what you need to succeed and grow."

Resolving "Identity Dysphoria" by Helping Kids Meet Five Core Needs

- **When they need direction:** "There are two things close to Jesus' heart: the Great Commandment and the Great Commission. The Great Commandment is to love God and love other people.[6] The Great Commission is to help other people want to obey God."[7]
- **When they need encouragement:** "Yesterday during that activity I noticed that you were really good at: organizing, giving instruction, encouraging, helping, or something else. I think God has gifted you for that."
- **When they struggle with life pursuits:** "I want you to have a job that you feel good about and that helps you take care of yourself and those around you. But having a good job won't make you a good person. It's important to find out what glorifies God and to not sin against him by ignoring what he says about us and about how we should live."
- **When they need to set an example:** "One thing I think is great about you is that you are humble and unselfish and you're not afraid to ask for help for yourself and those around you."

The wrong question is, "What will get me noticed?" Instead, compare the selfish, short-lived joy of being noticed to the deep and long-lasting joy of leaving the world a better place by serving, loving, and living an abundant life.

God answers the purpose question best. "Why am I alive?" I am alive to glorify God, put him on display, and become more like Jesus. Believers are God's workmanship. Strong in the Lord, we think in new ways, press on toward the goal of winning the prize of the high calling of God, are gifted to do good work, and have been washed, sanctified, and justified.[8]

Children will want the Triune God to meet their need for purpose if they see that you depend on all of God. Talk with children about how praise and worship fulfill our purpose and how activities like giving, reflecting, serving, praying, going to church, and honoring the Sabbath are helpful, too.

Core Need #5: Competence—What Do I Do Well?

Children need competence to accomplish their purpose and increase their self-security. Competence is healthiest when children rely on God, their character, and their decision-making, and work to develop their skills. When you help them become competent, you also bolster your position as a source of security, establishing you as a significant influence. Competence can motivate children to know their strengths, establish healthy belonging, live intentionally, and not give in to weaknesses.

Be wise so children can count on you as an excellent source of competence. Point them to God as their ultimate competence.

Take action: *Teach* them who they can be and what they can do so they will be competent; don't *tell* them. Increase the number of people they can trust and who they belong to, so they have many to turn to in times of need. Here are some ways to talk about competence with your children:

- **When they struggle for purpose:** "I hope you get lots of opportunities to win in your life but never forget that you aren't what you do. You're so much more than that. You're a child of the God who made the whole universe."
- **When they need to work harder:** "God has given you purpose, and he wants you to grow in it. That means working hard. Someone who is a gifted runner still has to practice and improve to honor God with their gift."
- **When they're comparing themselves to others:** "Asking 'How did other kids do?' can be helpful to make sure you're doing your best. But the goal isn't to be better than others; it is to be

everything God designed you to be."
- **When their priorities seem out of whack:** "The more I go in life the more I realize that the people who are most skilled aren't always the people who do best. The people who do best are the ones who are humble and teachable, show gratitude for what they have, and feel joy when they see other people do their best."

The wrong question is "What can I do perfectly?" So, talk about the unhealthy critical spirit this causes and children's need to grow, take risks, be resilient, and trust God and others during difficult times.

God answers the competence question best. "What can I do well?" As a believer, I can do all things through Christ, who strengthens me. (I cannot *be* all things, but I can *do* all things God wants me to do.) Believers have the mind of Christ and the power to control our thoughts. We are the temple of the Holy Spirit, overcomers, not afraid, and more.[9]

Children will want the Triune God to meet their need for competence if they see that you depend on all of God. Talk with children about hearing and following the Spirit and how relational activities like reading and memorizing Scripture, prayer, service, the church, and submitting can build competence.

TOUGH QUESTION: ARE YOU RELYING ON YOUR CHILDREN OR YOURSELF TO MEET YOUR CORE NEEDS?

Here's a challenging exercise. Go back, reread the chapter, and make it about you, not your children. You have the same core needs your children have, and God wants to meet them. We caution you against pressuring your children to meet your needs. We see this all the time when parents say:
- "I can trust my children. They'll never let me down." (security)

- "See those children over there? I get to be their parent!" (identity)
- "My children are my best friends!" (belonging)
- "Raising my children has been my greatest joy." (purpose)
- "I've been a good parent." (competence)

Please hear our hearts. Often, parents who find it especially hard to live with the life choices of their adult children are those who have tried to meet their own core needs through their children, and it hasn't gone well. God didn't bless you with children so they would meet your needs. No, *God* wants to meet your core needs! When he does, you can fully enjoy your role as a parent and engage well with your children without fear, stress, and burdening them by being needy.

Be careful of trying to meet your own core needs, too:

- "I don't need to trust anybody. I've got this." (security)
- "I'm a tough person. I can figure it out." (identity)
- "My kids need me even if they don't want me." (belonging)
- "I've got to fix this mess!" (purpose)
- "I've figured out every other crisis with my kids." (competence)

Can we suggest letting God meet your core needs, and praying the same for your children?

- **Security: Who can I trust?** "I can trust God to be a good Creator and faithful now because he has met my needs and answered my prayers in helpful ways so many times."
- **Identity: Who am I?** "I'm a Christ follower with strong faith who relies on God. I still sin sometimes, but I no longer define myself by my sin."
- **Belonging: Who wants me?** "I revel in my growing relationship with God because of his love."

Resolving "Identity Dysphoria" by Helping Kids Meet Five Core Needs

- **Purpose: Why am I alive?** "I'm alive to glorify God through who I am and what I do and that includes telling people about him and helping those who know him mature in their faith."
- **Competence: What do I do well?** "When I rely on God's power and strength and the leading of the Holy Spirit, he equips me to do what I should be doing."

We have all we need through God's life, purpose, presence, character, and instruction. As we read in Psalm 23:1, "The Lord is my shepherd; I shall not want." Identity confidence and gender confidence are very possible!

But at this point, you might be asking, "How, exactly, does belief in God help my kids become gender confident?" Great question. As it turns out, when we see God and the world as revealed in Scripture, it gives us a strong foundation of gender confidence that isn't shaken by cultural storms. Let's examine specifically how that's true in the next chapter.

DR. JEFF'S PERSPECTVE
GOOD WELDING GLORIFIES GOD

Most boys learn on their feet. It's one of the reasons my sons and I enjoyed touring factories as one of our favorite pastimes. We visited a soda bottling plant and tried a dozen different kinds of soda (which led to lots of hilarious burping), watched the construction of a fishing vessel, saw the fabrication of world-class trumpets, and followed the complex process of restoring World War 2 aircraft. If we saw a factory, we stopped in. Most didn't give official tours—we just asked someone to show us around.

Each tour taught us about craftsmanship. Once, we visited a liquid tanker-truck manufacturer. Our guide showed us two welds inside a tank.

Both met regulations, but one was lumpy and ugly and the other smooth and beautiful. He told us that one welder saw welding as his *job*, the other saw it as an *art*. These welds were inside a tank. *No one outside the factory would ever see them.* But God sees. Every weld is a chance to create something strong and safe that makes God smile.

I'm grateful that both boys approach their jobs today proud of their craftsmanship.

Download the Chapter Three resource, "God Answers Our Deepest Questions," at genderconfidentkids.com.

CHAPTER 4

HOW SCRIPTURE AND A BIBLICAL WORLDVIEW STRENGTHEN GENDER CONFIDENCE

We live in a world of confusion. When it comes to gender, our culture teaches children to celebrate their confusion rather than to seek clarity. They're encouraged to ignore the reality of male and female and instead see gender as fluid, self-assigned, changeable, or meaningless. These are all lies, and they're hurting our kids.

But as we've written, there *is* hope. And it is *not* found in airtight arguments, though it is essential to have good reasons for your beliefs. Instead, the best source of gender confidence is a biblical worldview that replaces confusion with clarity and transforms us by its truth.

A worldview is a lens through which we see the world. We humans are wired to make sense of things. A biblical worldview makes sense of things by relying on God as he is revealed in the Bible. God designed the world. He created us to take on his shape, not to shape ourselves. He gave us souls and organized our physical bodies to help us achieve His purposes.

> The Bible's teachings open the portal into reality itself.

For reasons we will explain in this chapter, we think the Bible's teachings open the portal into reality itself. The most important question from a biblical worldview is not, "*Who* am I?" but "*Whose* am I?" If we grasp that, it affects how we understand gender and everything else.

False worldviews, on the other hand, distort reality and create confusion. If your worldview tells you that you are the center of reality, you'll feel pressure to make every decision based on popularity, beauty, or performance. In our work with young adults, we've seen the devastating ways false worldviews lead to stress, anxiety, selfish priorities, and feelings of inferiority or judgmentalism. Gender confusion lies to us and says, "If only I can change my gender, then I'll be popular, beautiful, and accepted."

A BIBLICAL WORLDVIEW BRINGS CLARITY IN A BLURRY WORLD

As we mentioned in the last chapter, children are vulnerable to those who promise clarity through popularity, beauty, performance, or any other "thing." When voices shout that "gender is a spectrum," or "You can be whoever you feel like today," kids without a biblical worldview may quickly lose sight of what's true. So, they follow the crowd, fall into despair, or both.

How Scripture and a Biblical Worldview Strengthen Gender Confidence

The issue isn't just that children are confused. Without a biblical worldview, there is very little they can build on to get clarity. When children know that "male and female he created them" (Genesis 1:27) and that "God is not a God of confusion but of peace" (1 Corinthians 14:33), they have a framework that helps them recognize and reject cultural lies and then embrace truth.

Children living out of a biblical worldview will have better mental health, be more resilient, and be able to live confidently in a world of lies, knowing that what they have is better than what the culture offers. All of this leads to confidence and an even deeper trust in God.

A biblical worldview answers life's biggest questions correctly and in life-giving ways. The answers will be based on Scripture—the one true life-giving guide that doesn't change when we change or when those around us begin valuing the wrong things. For example:

- **Who am I?** You are made in the image of God, male or female, on purpose, with a purpose, and for a purpose.
- **What am I worth?** You are worth the life of Jesus, who gave Himself to redeem you.
- **Why do I feel broken?** You feel broken because sin has affected every part of creation, including your understanding of who you are and why you're here.
- **Can I be whole again?** By putting your faith in Jesus, you can be born all over again and get a fresh start. You can see the whole world clearly because you trust God.
- **What do I do when my feelings don't match God's truth?** You can patiently trust God anyway, knowing that he is making you stronger every day.

No worldview but the biblical one offers those answers, and certainly not with such love, logic, consistency, and hope. (Consider how children might answer these five questions if their worldview says that they, not God, are the center of reality.)

> A maturing biblical worldview isn't just in your head. It is in your heart and reflected in your habits.

A maturing biblical worldview isn't just in your head. It is in your heart and reflected in your habits. It becomes something you're aware of, that you feel some ownership of, and that changes how you process everything that happens to you.[1]

FIVE WAYS A BIBLICAL WORLDVIEW OFFERS GENDER CONFIDENCE

#1: It gives confidence a foundation.

When they look inside themselves, children find confusion, not confidence. Culture tells them to "follow their heart," but Scripture tells us the heart is deceitful.[2] Only the truth can stabilize them, and the Bible offers the only unshifting foundation for identity.

#2: It gives dignity based on God's design.

Our culture says identity is self-created. This is untrue, and exhausting. In contrast, God gives identity as a gift. When children understand they were formed by a loving Creator who made them male or female for his glory and their good, they breathe easier. Their gender becomes something to steward, not something to dismiss.

#3: It connects right belief and right behavior.

King David said of God, "For you formed my inward parts; you knitted me together in my mother's womb"(Psalm 139:13). When children understand that God's design is not random but purposeful, they start to live with purpose. When they trust God's authority, it helps them act with integrity. When they accept God's plan, they find joy in their design. A biblical worldview aligns what they believe with how they live.

#4: It harnesses emotions to serve the truth.

Without a biblical worldview, children are ruled by emotions. But when Scripture is their lens, they are equipped to step back, evaluate, and choose truth over impulse. Proverbs 29:11 says, "A fool gives full vent to his spirit, but a wise man quietly holds it back." We gain stability when we know that what God says is true and we patiently trust it. And stability brings confidence. Gender confusion mushrooms in the absence of truth, where unharnessed emotions reign.

#5: It meets children's core needs.

- **Security in their design** – They are not a mistake. Their bodies are not the problem. God's creation of them as male or female is intentional and good.
- **Authority to trust** – God's Word is a reliable guide. It doesn't change with the times and has been proven trustworthy across generations.
- **Purpose and clarity** – Gender is not just biological—it's missional. It connects to calling, community, and contribution in God's kingdom.
- **Freedom from cultural pressure** – They don't have to conform to trends or feelings. They are free to walk in truth with joy.
- **Resilience in the face of doubt** – Even when they feel out of place or unhappy, they have a firm framework.

WHAT HAPPENS WHEN CHILDREN BELIEVE AND TRUST GOD'S WORD

Many parents have shared that, "My kids don't believe the Bible is true, so I can't use it to convince them they're wrong about changing their gender." While it is correct that someone who doubts God's Word will find it hard to be confident in God and thus confident in their own design, we need to make an important observation. If children stop believing in the Bible, it isn't that they move from biblical belief to no belief at all. They simply shift their belief to another source of authority. What new authority is being trusted, and why? This is a meaningful conversation to have, especially with adult children.

If we didn't have the Bible, we could still discern that humans are male and female. But *why* God made male and female humans is something we can't accurately understand without the Bible's revelation about God and reality.

You probably want children to believe the Bible is true for several reasons. Most importantly, you want them to believe in and trust Jesus for their salvation. You want them to have a flourishing life based on God's principles. You want them to discover that living rightly isn't a burden; it's a blessing.

When children decide to trust the Bible because it's true, it changes how they see everything. They begin to see themselves as God sees them, not as victims of biology or culture, but as beloved image-bearers. The feeling that they need to scar themselves to be whole diminishes. Instead, they trust the One who made them, and that trust becomes the foundation of gender confidence. Gender confidence is not arrogance or rigidity, but a quiet, stable joy in being who God made them to be.

Gender confident children stop asking, "Who do I feel like today?" and start asking, "Who did God create me to be?" They stop believing the

How Scripture and a Biblical Worldview Strengthen Gender Confidence

lie that their body is a mistake and start believing they are "knitted together" on purpose by a loving Creator (Psalm 139:13). They stop chasing identity in trends or feelings and rest in the unchanging truth of God's design. When children believe the Bible is true, it settles their identity. And when their identity is settled, they can confidently live on purpose and contribute in beautiful and meaningful ways, further building their delight and confidence.

> **Confidence is the fruit of truth, rooted in love, and harvested in peace.**

Confidence is the fruit of truth, rooted in love, and harvested in peace. We've seen it repeatedly: Many children who once questioned their identity stand tall when they understand who God is and who they are in him.

So, how do kids learn to believe the Bible and accept its truth? Our colleagues who teach at Summit Ministries have written many great resources, including curricula for all ages. We like Natasha Crain's podcast and book, *Talking with Your Kids About God: 30 Conversations Every Christian Parent Must Have*,[3] and the excellent work of Hilary Morgan Ferrer and the team at Mama Bear Apologetics.[4] But let's review the basics here.

HERE ARE JUST FIVE REASONS—AMONG MANY—WHY CHILDREN CAN TRUST THE BIBLE

The Bible is not just a book; it's the inspired Word of God. When we speak to students in Christian schools, we implore them to view the Bible as more than another textbook. It's a collection of writings by over 40 authors over 1,500 years, written in multiple languages and cultures, yet telling one unified story: God's plan to redeem His people through Jesus. It's a miraculous book, and there's strong evidence that it is true:

- **Historical Accuracy** – Archaeology and ancient records confirm the accuracy of the people, places, and events described in Scripture.

- **Prophetic Fulfillment** – Hundreds of prophecies in the Old Testament were fulfilled in the life, death, and resurrection of Jesus.
- **Consistency** – Despite being written by many different people over centuries, the Bible has one inspired, cohesive message.
- **Preservation** – No book in history has been copied, preserved, and distributed more accurately or widely than the Bible.
- **Transformational Power** – Despite fierce criticism, the Bible has exerted more of a positive influence on society than any other book, especially when it comes to treating people with dignity. It's changed the lives of billions and continues to do so.

Children can trust the Bible because it's been proven trustworthy. And more than that, it's living and active.[5] It speaks to their hearts today just as it has for millennia.

Without the Bible, kids are left to culture's confusing messages about identity, worth, and gender. That's dangerous because, as we've identified here, the culture doesn't love our kids; it feeds on them.

But God does love them. And his Word gives them the truth that leads to life and freedom.[6]

HOW YOU CAN HELP CHILDREN TRUST THE BIBLE AND BUILD A BIBLICAL WORLDVIEW

How do we help kids trust the Bible—really trust it—in a way that strengthens them against the pressure to question their design or reinvent themselves? How do we raise children who believe that God's Word is not only true but also *good*, and that it applies to *them*?

The answer lies in **intentional discipleship** and **individual understanding**. We need to lay the groundwork for belief in a way that connects to who they are, and how they think, feel, and experience the world.

Kathy's insights on children's *eight smarts* help connect discipleship and understanding. Each child is smart in different ways, and different kinds of smartness offer a doorway into belief through words, music, logic, nature, self-reflection, physical movement, visual learning, or social interaction. The question isn't, "How smart am I?" but "How am I smart?" We've seen many students at Summit Ministries gain confidence in God's design, including for their gender, when they realize that he is a loving heavenly Father who made them smart in ways the world really needs.[7]

> Children need to see other people living confidently in their God-given identity. Every child benefits from witnessing faith in action.

One more thing. When discipling children, please remember the broader circle of community. We don't disciple children alone. Children need to see other people living confidently in their God-given identity. Let them hear testimonies of people who once struggled with their identity but now walk in peace. Every child benefits from witnessing faith in action.

HOW TO HAVE MEANINGFUL CONVERSATIONS BASED ON A BIBLICAL WORLDVIEW

Our lives are a textbook our children read to discern what is important. As they see us making decisions based on the Bible, they'll learn to rely on God through prayer and his Word. As they see us humble ourselves, they'll learn to rely on God through repentance.

Conversing well is one of the most important things we can model. Children need space to express their doubts, especially around big topics like identity and gender. When a child asks, "Why did God make me this way?" or "What if I don't feel like a girl today?" they're not just looking for quick answers—they're looking for safety. If we panic or dismiss their questions, they may hide their struggles or turn to Google or TikTok. But if we stay calm, ask thoughtful questions, and explore Scripture with them, it demonstrates that doubt isn't dangerous when brought into the light.

To this end, please consider these recommendations:

- **Prioritize children over ideas.** Before you teach them, children need to know that you see them, love them, and want to help them. Arguing about gender ideology can be counterproductive; we've known children whose primary motivation became to prove their parents wrong. What we're looking for is a life change, not a quarrel. Say, "I don't want to turn this into a debate where we just find ammunition to shoot at each other. I want to see you honor God and reach your full potential."
- **Prioritize listening.** This book offers dozens of question suggestions, but the base question on gender confusion is, "Can you help me understand?" We want children to know we're really listening, not just waiting for our turn to talk. Be an active listener and nod, make and maintain eye contact, and verbally acknowledge them without taking over the conversation. Quick comments like "That makes sense" and "I see" can motivate them to keep sharing.
- **Start now.** The sooner you show yourself as someone your children can talk to about anything, the more authority you'll have when tough topics arise. Say, "The people on the internet may seem smart, but they don't know you like God knows you. They don't see how you're special. They don't really think through how their words affect people and make them feel unsafe."
- **Be present.** Put your phone down, be present and available, and talk with your children when they want to (as much as you can). If you haven't been in the habit of doing this but want to begin, consider saying, "I'm so sorry I've been distracted when

we're trying to talk about important things. I'm going to put my phone in the other room and work on listening more carefully." And you've got to mean it!
- **Commit to ongoing conversations, not one-and-done discussions.** Take advantage of teachable moments on serious topics like faith, identity, and gender, but also about fun topics, so they don't assume that every conversation must be serious. Say, "I'm really interested in knowing how you see this." Or, if your child is shy about sharing opinions, say, "I'm really interested in knowing how other people your age see this."
- **Don't always insist on eye contact.** Children have told us they don't want to see their parents' or teachers' faces if they think they'll be disappointed, sad, or scared. Instead, walk and talk. Talk in the car. Talk in the dark. Boys especially prefer shoulder-to-shoulder conversations while doing something or going somewhere.
- **Ask about feelings, thoughts, and actions.** "How do you feel about that?" "What do you think about that?" "What action did you take, or do you want to take?" If there's inconsistency between their feelings, thoughts, and actions, point that out. Say, "When you feel strongly about something but aren't willing to act, I'm confused. I'd like to talk about how to make sure your feelings, thoughts, and actions are lined up with the truth."
- **Feel their feelings before suggesting solutions.** Feelings and thoughts go together. "God cares about how we feel and how we think. When we put him first, he gives us peace that we're doing the right thing." If you know they're confused, you can say, "I'm sorry this is so confusing, because confusion doesn't feel safe. Let's ask God to help make it clear."

- **Use open-ended questions.** Open-ended questions help you get as much of a child's story or concern as possible before sharing your thoughts. The problem with confusing topics like gender is that they are, well, confusing. And confusing things are hard to talk about. Just like it takes time and patience to paint a picture, it takes time and patience to make sense of things by talking them out. Make statements like, "Tell me more," "Please keep talking; I want to hear your thoughts," and "I want to understand." A good follow-up question is, "Is there anything else you'd like to share?"
- **Before offering solutions, ask what they believe would be best.** It inspires confidence and trust if you can affirm at least some of what your child is saying. If you believe something is unwise, first ask, "Help me understand why you think that's a good idea." That way, you'll know *how* they're thinking, not just *what* they think. As you do this, don't be afraid to boldly correct their false thinking and tell them what would be better and why.
- **Appropriately share your feelings without manipulation.** You have a right to be disappointed at how things are going, but an open posture is better than a closed one. "This is not God's best for you" is better than "You should be ashamed of yourself." "I want you to hear my heart about what is true" is better than "You were taught better than that."
- **Be confident in God's truth.** When we show how God shapes our thoughts and desires, our children will learn to trust God's Word over other people's opinions. Be careful of answering questions with "In my opinion . . . " and "I think . . . " If you decide based on opinions, you encourage children to do the same thing.

Instead, use statements like: "Based on Scripture . . . ", "God's Word teaches . . . ", "I've studied Scripture and prayed about this and concluded that . . . ", and "I've had a lot of experience with this, and here's what I've learned . . . " Open the Bible with them and explore together. If you aren't sure how to do that, we recommend talking with your pastor and consulting articles from websites like summit.org, gotquestions.org, and focusonthefamily.com.

A BIBLICAL WORLDVIEW SAYS "YOU ARE NOT A MISTAKE"

As we do these things—starting now, modeling caring, explaining the biblical roots of belief, welcoming questions, and surrounding kids with a truth-filled community—we're not just raising Bible readers. We're raising Bible *believers*.

And when children believe the Bible is true, they begin to believe that they are *not* a mistake. They no longer need to reinvent themselves to fit in or feel safe, popular, beautiful, or perfect. They see that being a boy or a girl is part of God's good plan. Their body isn't broken. Their identity isn't up for grabs. Who they are—male or female—is part of their purpose, not something they need to figure out or fight for.

This is gender confidence, not confidence in themselves, but confidence in the One who made them. And that kind of confidence changes everything.

Culture offers a thousand identities. Scripture offers one: child of God, fearfully and wonderfully made, male or female by design. That's not limiting. That's liberating.

If we want children to walk confidently in the bodies God gave them, we must lead them to embrace a biblical worldview. It is the lens through which gender confusion fades, and gender confidence grows.

> **Culture offers a thousand identities. Scripture offers one.**

Without a biblical worldview, the ground beneath them will shake. With it, they will stand strong, anchored in truth, secure in design, and confident in their Creator. We need the Bible's truth now more than ever, especially as we unmask culture's lies about gender and gain confidence that Scripture responds to them with authoritative truth. That's what we'll examine next.

⬇ Looking for more on the reliability of the Bible? Download the Chapter Four resource, "Raising Kids Who Trust the Bible," at genderconfidentkids.com.

CHAPTER 5

FOUR BIBLICAL TRUTHS THAT REFUTE FOUR CULTURAL LIES ABOUT GENDER

Lies about gender are everywhere, and they're taking our children down. Children must know the truth so they can discern when they're being lied to. You and I need to know it, too. Thankfully, the Bible offers clear, dependable, complete, and understandable truth.

So that you and your children can understand God's planned differences between genders and how they harmonize, we'll look at the creation account, the Old Testament the New Testament, and the biblical context.

Our goal isn't to settle the debate about gender roles in the Bible. It's to see what the Bible reveals about our created purpose so we can rise above gender confusion.

After examining God's truths, we'll explain four major lies the culture tells about gender. These lies are dangerous because they *create* confusion that they then "fix" in a way that doesn't honor God. We know they're frustrating to think about, but we need to understand these lies so we and our children can see the beauty of the truth and wholeheartedly embrace it. We pray that by looking at what the culture gets wrong, you'll be better equipped to strengthen your children's thinking, feelings, and decisions.

Truth #1: Male and Female in Creation

God designed humans to bear his image and likeness.[1] Genesis 1:27 explains that God made humans as male (in Hebrew, *zakar* connotes masculinity) and female (*neqebah* signifies femininity). The categories of *male* and *female* have created purposes. They aren't just roles that people play.

Not to geek out too much on biblical languages, but *zakar* and *negebah* imply both physiological and psychological purposes. Males and females are different in ways that create harmony, bringing out the best in each. In Genesis 2:18, God says about the man, "I will make a helper suitable for him." The term *suitable* means "in the sight of, or opposite to." The term *helper* (from the Hebrew word *ezer*) means a rescuer or completer.

In woman, God made a powerful rescuer who stood opposite the man, completing God's design for both. Just as two pitches of a roof create strength by holding each other in tension, the man and the woman work together for God's glory. All the Bible's opposites—light and dark, day and night, land and sea—display the harmony of God's design. This is a beautiful truth to share with children.

God didn't make male and female opposites to attack each other, but to help each other abound. We're sure you've been blessed with healthy

Four Biblical Truths that Refute Four Cultural Lies About Gender

friendships and working relationships with people of the opposite gender, and you want this for children, too. The harmonizing is especially true in marriage. Together, the man and the woman become "*one flesh*" (literally, "to *flesh, one*"). This kind of oneness displays God's image to the world.

As leadership speaker and author Vince Miller pointed out on a Summit Ministries podcast, because we have male and female, we also can have fathers and mothers, brothers and sisters, and sons and daughters. All these relationships point to the fatherhood of God.[2]

Every culture develops stereotypes around males and females. Stereotypes control us by limiting and freezing our perceptions of each other. Believers should instead focus on and celebrate the purposes of God's design. We call these purposes *imagotypes* because they are based on the *Imago Dei*, which is Latin for *image of God*. When we celebrate God's design, we aren't controlled by human-created patterns but we're free and transformed by the renewing of our minds.[3]

If you're a follower of Jesus, you should never feel the need to apologize for God's purposeful design. Because God created us *on* purpose, we get to live *with* purpose. The culture loves a "battle of the sexes" that pits males and females against each other. But in God's design, males and females are *for* each other and for a purpose greater than either could achieve alone. Make sure your children know this!

> **Because God created us on purpose, we get to live with purpose.**

But there's more. God created you with a soul as well as with a body. A soul is what it's like to be you, enabling you to sense things, have beliefs and desires, and act with purpose. Your soul guides what you do and is shaped by what you do. Male and female souls are similar in many ways, but different in others. For instance, Scripture tells us all to avoid rage. Males, whose biology responds to threats more impulsively, experience rage differently than women, who respond to threats more through decision-making. This doesn't mean that males or females have better souls, but it does indicate that gender differences are soul-deep. This is another reason gender can't be changed with medicine or damaging surgical procedures. Gender is more than physical. Talk to your children about this.

Truth #2: The Old Testament and Gender

Many people find the Old Testament offensive to modern sensibilities. They view whatever it says about males and females as irrelevant. This is a tremendous mistake. If we ignore the Old Testament, we'll radically misunderstand how the Bible applies to our lives today. Not to mention how it sets the stage for Jesus' entry into the story. We need it!

Some see the Old Testament as anti-woman. The British law professor Jonathan Burnside dispenses with this notion. In his exhaustive study, he shows that many Old Testament laws revolve around *protecting* women and children.[4]

Take, for example, the test required of a woman whose husband suspected her of adultery. The woman was brought before the priests and made to drink a concoction mixed with dust from the tabernacle floor. Some people say, "What a demeaning thing to do! The Bible is so out of touch."

But this passage isn't about humiliating women. It is about protecting them. In the nations surrounding Israel, men who suspected their wives of misconduct often killed them and got away with it. It still happens in many places around the world today. The Old Testament law *protected* wives by taking the decision to punish them out of their husbands' hands. It ended a horrid practice.

Other people say, "The Old Testament demeans women by not allowing them to be priests." However, as Jewish radio talk show host Dennis Prager points out in his commentary on the book of Numbers, women in the Old Testament *were* allowed to be prophets, which is a spiritually higher calling. So, it can't just be about men being in charge and leaving women out. Prager speculates that the purpose of having male priests may have been to desexualize religion. In surrounding cultures, temples were overseen by female prostitutes. Men took advantage of these women to make themselves feel more spiritual.[5]

Women and children suffer when men worship sex. By making the priesthood exclusive to men, perhaps Moses was setting up a system where men could aspire to manhood not by being sexually active, but by being godly. No other religious system we know about was structured in this way and for this purpose.

You and your children may have many other questions about Old Testament practices. It's not the purpose of this book to grapple with them all, but to show that when we view the Bible in light of God's relationship with humanity, we see that it elevates both females and males. Share this section with your children to help them see how understanding Scripture clarifies how to feel, think, and act today.

Truth #3: The New Testament and Gender

Jesus affirmed the Old Testament teachings about gender. He said, "Haven't you read . . . that at the beginning the Creator made them male and female?" (Matthew 19:4). Jesus used the differences between males and females to highlight the importance of faithful marital relationships. The Apostle Paul, in turn, used marriage to illustrate how God's design of males and females expands our vision of Christ and the church. These visions elevate both marriage and singleness. They show that our deepest fulfillment should be found in our identity as redeemed followers of Jesus, rather than as merely sexual creatures responding to evolutionary urges.

Despite the New Testament's high view of humanity, many criticize it as a diatribe designed to put women down. Passages like 1 Timothy 2 receive special scrutiny. In this difficult passage, Paul instructs women in the church at Ephesus not to distinguish themselves with jewelry or have authority over a man, but to learn in quietness. The word used is the Greek word *hesuchia*, which means a state of tranquility. *Strong's Bible Dictionary* describes this virtue as "an ideal state for philosophers and those seeking wisdom."[6]

Is this a universal call for women not to teach men? Many Christian traditions say "yes." We're not going to settle this debate here. If you're hoping for insight into whether your daughter may aspire to a pastoral role, this is not the book for you. This book is mostly about purposes, not roles.

Women were vital to Jesus's ministry and that of the apostles. A biblical worldview is boundary-breaking in that it gives men and women, Jews and gentiles, slaves and free people the opportunity to harmonize and help each other grow spiritually.[7]

Truth #4: The Context Matters

When Jeff was a child, he heard a sermon about hippie hair. The pastor instructed men to cut their hair short, quoting from 1 Corinthians 11:14: "Does not nature itself teach you that if a man wears long hair it is a disgrace for him?" "Jesus doesn't like hippie hair," the pastor stated.

Jeff remembers this vividly because at that moment he thought of a drawing he had seen of Jesus with . . . hippie hair. (You've seen it too, right?!) Even as a child, it seemed evident to him that the pastor hadn't really addressed what Jesus thought about such a thing. He, the pastor, didn't like hippie hair and found a text to prove his point.

At Summit Ministries, we help students go deep into biblical texts by asking them to study what these texts would have meant to their original hearers. Often, core principles emerge that we miss through a cursory glance.

As Brandon Showalter and Jeff show in their book *Exposing the Gender Lie*,[8] it is evident from many ancient sources that Greek men commonly

Four Biblical Truths that Refute Four Cultural Lies About Gender

preferred effeminate boys to women. Older, powerful men publicly preyed on vulnerable young men who were of lesser status. Often, young men saw submitting to this abuse as a path to social advancement.

> Scripture rejects the predatory practices of surrounding cultures and displays a vision of the harmony between males and females.

The church in Corinth, a city famous for its sexual immorality, might well have seen this text about long hair in that light. It is inappropriate for men to pretend to be the opposite sex for a manifestly sinful purpose. Today, hairstyles are mostly neutral. It's not about hippie hair. It's about a man's identity based on God's design. It's also about protecting marital relationships so that lifelong devotion develops between a man and a woman. It was literally a turning point in the history of civilization that benefits us to this day.[9]

Throughout its pages, Scripture rejects the predatory practices of surrounding cultures and displays a vision of the harmony between males and females that protects families, which in turn stabilizes communities, enables economic flourishing,[10] and promotes spiritual growth.

HOW FALSE WORLDVIEWS AND DISTORTIONS HARM BOYS AND GIRLS, MEN AND WOMEN

Opposite of a biblical worldview, false worldviews *worsen* the relationship between males and females. In the teachings of Buddha, for example, women are seen as a source of pollution.[11] The only way for females to achieve enlightenment is to be reincarnated as males. (Depending on your children's maturity, you could study other worldviews with them to show how God's elevated view of men and women compares.)

And while some altogether reject a biblical worldview of gender, others twist a biblical worldview in a way that turns it into a harmful weapon. In a spirit of humble repentance, we must recognize that a biblical worldview of gender is broken everywhere, even in the church. Nearly every time we travel to speak, we meet women who won't go to church because they experienced abuse at the hands of a predatory male masquerading as a Christian. Such abuse is an abhorrent affront to God and His image-bearers. Too, we meet men who feel that church is geared to the spiritual needs of women, and that men have no place. This, too, is a travesty.

We pray you'll help children understand God and his ways according to his Word and not how some Christians or some churches behave.

DO YOU BELIEVE ANY OF THESE LIES ABOUT GENDER? DO YOUR CHILDREN?

Now that we've examined why the Bible's truth matters, we are ready to unmask popular culture's lies. Popular culture stubbornly refuses to admit that our design has purpose. Instead, it promotes one counterfeit view of gender after another. We'll look at four of them.

Chances are, you've heard of one or more of these counterfeit views of gender. You may have even mistakenly believed one of them. It is a virtual certainty that each of these lies has influenced children. Children did not think them up, but children are their primary victims. These lies were invented by adults who ought to have known better but sadly want to manipulate children and encourage confusion. You'll see that each lie begins with rejecting God and ends in disaster.

Lie #1: "I'm Trapped in the Wrong Body."

Many gender-insecure people speak of being "trapped in the wrong body." Why don't people talk about being "trapped in the wrong soul"? Because it is assumed that our souls are the true "us," and that our bodies keep us from being set free.

Four Biblical Truths that Refute Four Cultural Lies About Gender

"Souls good, bodies bad" is an ancient heresy called Gnosticism, which says that our souls are what matters and that our bodies are of secondary importance. Today, Gnosticism is often called *transhumanism*. According to neuroethics professor Fabrice Jotterand, transhumanism posits "that the body is totally irrelevant to our identity as a human being" and that "the body becomes something you can manipulate at will and doesn't have any normative stand in defining who we are as human beings."[12]

> Our bodies are an essential part of our design.

The Bible rejects Gnosticism in whatever form. Jesus came in a body (see John 1). He took on flesh and lived among us. Philippians 3:21 explains that Christ will "transform our lowly body to be like his glorious body." Romans 8:23 speaks of the "redemption of our bodies."

Our bodies are an essential part of our design, as we saw in Truth #1 about gender and creation, not a prison in which we are trapped. They help us glorify God.[13] The Bible treats our gender as a good part of God's design, integral to how we worship God and grow spiritually.

Lie #2: "Gender Falls on a Spectrum."

The wildly popular idea of the "gender spectrum" suggests that male and female are just distinctions on two far ends of a scale. Most people aren't either G.I. Joe or LeBron James or Barbie or Taylor Swift, so what is "normal" isn't male or female.

When illustrated, the gender spectrum lists attributes like *courage* as "masculine" and *sensitivity* as "feminine." So, if you're a courageous woman, you may be more male than female. And if you're a sensitive male, you may be more female than male. The gender spectrum has convinced many that they were born in the wrong body because they don't match hyper-masculine or hyper-feminine traits.

Where do the attributes on the spectrum come from? Advocates say that they are based on society's perceptions. But *whose* perceptions? A strong majority believes that gender is binary, not a spectrum of varying levels of transgenderism, so it can't be *their* perceptions. Is it based on scientific research? No. As we've mentioned, scientists have identified 6,500 physiological differences between males and females.[14]

When it comes down to it, gender-spectrum advocates enshrine *their* stereotypes as facts and then use those supposed facts to generate the perception that society's perceptions are misguided. If you look at gender spectrum writings long enough, you'll realize why. Gender spectrum advocates see men as a threat. They fear a "patriarchy" in which men control the desirable forms of power. This patriarchy, they say, is the root of all evil. If you can rid society of the idea of "man" or "woman," you can neuter men and make the world a better place.

As we saw in Truth #2 about gender and the Old Testament, the Bible lifts up women, setting in place principles that protect their dignity and reigning in the ungodly impulses men display when they're not focused on God.

Lie #3: "My Sexuality is my Main Identity."

While some in the transgender movement say that our bodies are *not* important, others say that they are the *only* important thing. This lie says that our sexual impulses, arising from strong biochemical reactions, are what make us authentically human.

The work of the Austrian psychoanalyst Sigmund Freud is often used to bolster this view. By putting sexual desire at the center of what makes us human, Freud spawned cynicism about social conventions that make sexuality private rather than public.

Four Biblical Truths that Refute Four Cultural Lies About Gender

The term *cynicism* goes back to an ancient Greek philosophical group, the Cynics, who taught that humans are reasoning animals. They rejected any cultural practice that constrained their innate animalism, especially as it related to sexuality.

Cynics have found new life in the sexual revolution, which mocks modest sensibility as backward because it prevents people from being "true to themselves."

Is it working? Nope. Today, people are less satisfied in their sexuality and everything else than ever before. Believing the lie that only our bodies matter has led to what Sara Rimer hauntingly describes as "anorexia of the soul."[15]

The Bible encourages us to set our minds on higher things.[16] It admonishes us to use our freedom not as an opportunity for the flesh, but to serve others.[17] Jesus didn't come to be served, but to serve[18] and we are to follow his example.[19] Fulfilling our bodily desires isn't the purpose of life. Love and service are. This includes our sexuality, which was lovingly designed by God and is good within the boundaries he has created.

> Our primary identity isn't in our sexuality, but in Jesus.

As we saw in Truth #3 about gender and the New Testament, our primary identity isn't in our sexuality, but in Jesus. And that positions us to see the value of others so we can serve them and help them grow.

Lie #4: "Gender is Just a Performance."

In the last half of the twentieth century, a movement in sociology reframed gender not as male and female traits rooted in biology, but as the performing of roles based on what we think is expected of us. Gender is about what we *do*, not who we *are*, this lie says. So *boy*, *girl*, *husband*, or *wife* are not meaningful distinctions. They're just labels given to people who are performing how they think they should act, based on what they think others expect of them.

This shift in thinking about gender spread like a virus through jargon-laden academic articles, such as a 1987 paper called "Doing Gender." Its authors rejected gender as a biological state and referred to it instead as a "routine accomplishment embedded in everyday interaction."[20] The paper reframed categories of male and female as relevant only in that we *present* ourselves as how we think male and female ought to be presented, based on the stereotypes we unconsciously accept.

Do you see the problem? If gender is just a performance, why would we care if biological males want to join women's sports teams or use women's restrooms? If most people can be made to think of these things as normal, then they are. No one can reasonably object to giving children high-powered and untested hormones to "change genders" if gender is merely a performance. But, as we've seen in Truth #4 about how context matters, the core principles arising from Scripture don't present gender as a performance but as an aspect of our design that needs to be carefully stewarded for spiritual growth and societal flourishing.

STAY FOCUSED ON IMAGOTYPES, NOT STEREOTYPES

The Bible gives us clarity and confidence about gender. Even though it was written long ago, it faithfully tells us who God is and who we are as his image-bearers. The culture tells lies to get us to reject this truth. But as we've seen, God designed males and females on purpose, with purpose. We harmonize with each other.

The Bible's imagotypes, based on God's image, rise above culture's stereotypes. They show that courage and sensitivity aren't two ends of a supposed gender spectrum, but character qualities that both males and females should embrace. The same is true for all other godly attributes. Character

Four Biblical Truths that Refute Four Cultural Lies About Gender

traits don't push us to one end or the other of a one-dimensional gender spectrum. They dwell in a higher dimension, defined by our relationship with God.

Focus on building character in your children, rather than worrying about cultural stereotypes. If your son likes to wear a pink shirt or play with stuffed animals, that doesn't make him a girl. If your daughter likes video games and trucks, that doesn't make her a boy. Girls can prefer helping dad fix things, and boys can enjoy helping mom in the kitchen. Boys can enjoy watching musicals with their grandmothers. Girls can enjoy watching Westerns with their grandfathers. None of these things makes us male and female. *God* makes us male and female. The embracing of a supposed gender spectrum has led to much bullying and gender confusion.

> Focus on building character in your children, rather than worrying about cultural stereotypes.

Kathy has advised many parents to let boys wear pink shirts if they like them. But if they're teased for liking pink, don't make them wear pink. It just isn't a battle worth fighting. Boys can sleep with a teddy bear, and if they don't want to go to a sleepover because they may be teased, that's okay. If girls don't want friends to know they help dad change the oil, don't make a big deal out of it.

We want you to know it's going to be okay. You can say something like this to your child: "Part of growing up is that kids tease each other, and sometimes it gets mean. I want you to believe what *God* says about you! God knows you better than your friends, and he loves you more. But if the teasing gets out of hand or someone makes you feel scared, will you tell me so I can help make it right?"

Alright. We've covered a lot of ground in discussing how a biblical worldview and Scripture respond to culture's lies. But how, specifically, do we help boys and girls become gender confident based on their design?

We're glad you asked, because that is exactly what we're going to focus on in the next two chapters, starting with boys.

DR. KATHY'S PERSPECTIVE
THE SOUL MATTERS!

Psalm 139:13–14 is a psalm of David containing a life-changing thought that relates to the gender discussion. We learn here that God formed our inward parts and we've been knit together in our mother's womb. I love encouraging children with these truths. They are who they are supposed to be! God creates each person intentionally and strategically, including their gender.

David continues in verse 14 by declaring, "Wonderful are your works; my soul knows it very well." Even though I'm a woman, my low voice causes some people to call me "sir" when I'm on the phone or ordering at the menu of a drive-thru restaurant. As you can imagine, this can be awkward and frustrating. Yet, I know who I am—a woman with a low voice. And because it's the voice God chose for me, I know it's right.

Some of the best radio and podcast hosts and producers have told me I have "a perfect voice." Low voices carry further than high voices. They can be heard above audience noise. Men prefer to listen to a woman with a low voice. Low voices convey authority.

My voice wasn't an issue until transgender became an issue. My love for God helped me to gain strength and confidence in his design. Part of my passion for this project stems from this. As I tell my audiences, if I were young today, being called "sir" might make me wonder if my low voice was right and everything else about me was wrong. Many years ago, while processing this, I woke up with Psalm 139:14 on my mind, and I knew deep down in my soul that my voice was perfect for me because my perfect Creator chose it for me. The issue was settled. Peace, joy, and confidence reign. The soul matters!

> We need to be critical thinkers to navigate a world of lies. Download the Chapter Five resource, "Thrive in a World of Lies," at genderconfidentkids.com.

CHAPTER 6

GUIDING BOYS TO BECOME CONFIDENT MEN BY USING THE CORE NEEDS

The mom was utterly baffled. "My boys . . . I don't understand them. *At all.* They can get into so much trouble, so fast. It's like they're not even thinking."

"Did you have brothers growing up?"

"No, only sisters."

"You know what, mom? You're not crazy and you're not alone. Your boys are totally normal."

The mom's face showed relief as she realized that while raising sons is a privilege, it is a very different undertaking than raising daughters.

This chapter is about raising godly sons who are confident in their God-designed gender. God has given boys the superpowers they need to live godly lives, yet they live in a culture that mocks masculinity. We're thinking of the insurance company whose series of commercials, "Backup," featured wives calling in studly NFL quarterbacks to do jobs their hapless husbands were too inept to complete.

In schools, boys are seen as disruptive or inattentive. We've talked to young men denied recess in elementary school because they could not sit still in class. Girls enjoy recess; boys need it!

Getting boys to fit an educational mold that doesn't suit them has consequences. In the years since the COVID-19 pandemic, diagnoses of ADHD have skyrocketed, with boys being twice as likely to be diagnosed as girls.[1] Certainly, good medical care has its place, but why are we so intent on "fixing" boys to fit the needs of the education system rather than fixing the education system to fit the needs of boys as well as girls?

ARE BOYS A THREAT OR A BLESSING?

It's uncomfortable to admit this, but our culture operates on a widespread belief that boys are bad. They're like pit bulls, cute when puppies but threatening when grown. One self-described progressive and feminist author found herself distressed at the allergic reaction her like-minded friends had to her sons. "My tribe is abandoning my kids," she realized.[2]

"It's a bad time to be a boy in America," says feminist scholar Christina Hoff Sommers.[3] Look at the top songs and shows. What is the vision of manhood that culture communicates? It's rarely positive, that's for sure. Boys are left to fend for themselves in knowing how to become men. Harvard political science professor Harvey Mansfield commented, gloomily,

"The problem of manliness is not that it does not exist. It does exist, but it is unemployed."[4]

Still, we see hopeful trends. As *New York Times* reporter Ruth Graham has documented, young men are far more likely than young women to identify as evangelicals. They are far less likely to identify as "nones" (those who mark "none" on surveys of religious preference). They're more interested in getting married and having kids. We may be witnessing the first time in recorded history that young men are more tuned into faith and family than young women are.[5]

To some, the rise of religiosity among young men signals doom. The patriarchy is rising once again, columnist Jill Fililpovic believes, and this "imperils men and women alike."[6] But, we need to ask, as Professor Nancy Pearcey does in a recent book, when does the war against toxic masculinity metastasize into a toxic war on masculinity?[7]

> We desperately need godly men. If we don't form them, society will deform them.

What can parents do? In her book *Moms Raising Sons to be Men*, Rhonda Stoppe eloquently states: "As strongly as I know how, I want to encourage you to make a conscious effort to show your son that you see him becoming a man—or he will fight you to prove it."[8]

History's greatest explorers have been men. For millennia, men have fought for truth and stood against injustice. We think of missionaries like Jim Eliot, who, with four colleagues, gave his life trying to reach out to a remote tribe in South America. Eliot wrote in his diary, "He is no fool to give what he cannot keep, to gain what he cannot lose."[9]

We think of Summit Ministries graduate Marc Lee, who became the first Navy SEAL to die in Operation Desert Shield. Marc gave his life shielding members of his SEAL team from an Iraqi ambush.

We desperately need godly men. If we don't form them, society will deform them. They can become into destroyers rather than defenders. More

Guiding Boys to Become Confident Men by Using the Core Needs

than 90% of prison inmates are men.[10] Nearly all terrorists are young men.[11] And it's not just men on the margins. It was Germany's elite men—half of whom had doctorates—who cast their lot with the devil and planned the mass murder of Jews.[12]

It is easier to get the man out of boyhood than the boyhood out of the man. Boys' bodies grow up even if their souls remain immature. Charged with testosterone and longing for significance, boys can become a blessing or a burden. They can shape culture or annihilate themselves. A healthy society responds to this challenge by channeling masculinity for cultural good, but an unhealthy society feels threatened by masculinity and seeks to turn men into non-men, obscuring the signposts leading to healthy manhood.

Boys need the strong guiding influence of older men to rise to maturity. Observing our students at Summit Ministries, we can instantly tell which ones have a masculinizing relationship with their fathers. They have an assured bearing. They make eye contact. They put others first.

Of course, many young men display these positive traits in the absence of involved fathers. But the exception proves the rule. All mature young men can point to the influence of an older man—a grandfather, coach, teacher, boss, or neighbor—who modeled how to be a man.

In Chapter Three, we showed that the most confident kids are those whose five core needs are met by God and nurtured by their parents and caregivers. Moms and dads can help their sons rise to godly maturity by tuning in to every young man's core needs:

- Who can I trust? (the core need for security)
- Who am I? (the core need for identity)
- Who wants me? (the core need for belonging)
- Why am I alive? (the core need for purpose)
- What do I do well? (the core need for competence)

Let's talk about how to unleash godly masculinity in each of these five areas.

Security: Who Can I Trust? Unleashing the Sage

The first core need is security. Boys ask, "Who can I trust?" We envision young men who look up to men who *expend* themselves for good causes and *expand* their world to help others grow.

When forming a biblical worldview, wisdom is shown by actions, not just beliefs. What we habitually do forms our public character. In Sunday School, we shouldn't be content teaching boys to make a coloring of Noah's ark. We should instead fascinate them with the full color of who Noah was, a man so bold that he toiled for decades at a task that earned him nothing but mockery.

> It isn't just about what they build. It's about who they build it with.

Similarly, we need to let boys grapple with how to become men like Paul, who never gave up no matter how tough things got, and like David, who had to learn to make things right after a terrible sin.

Jesus said in Matthew 7 that those who hear his words and act on them will be like a wise man who built his house on the rock. Those who hear his words and don't act on them will be like a foolish man who built his house on the sand. Life's rains and winds don't shape your character; they reveal it.

Boys' brains are wired to act first and think later.[13] Sometimes they do dumb things in the process of learning to be smart. Boys need to know that their life's work will be on public display, whether they build rightly or wrongly.

And it isn't just about what they build. It's about who they build it with. Scripture says "a companion of fools suffers harm" (Proverbs 13:20). The Bible narrates the life of Rehoboam, son of Solomon, who caused a civil war by ignoring wise counsel and seeking the approval of foolish peers.[14] How many kingdoms, families, and businesses have been split by failure to heed wise counsel!

Even when they're young, boys can tell the difference between wise and foolish friends. Wise friends show respect to others. Foolish friends show contempt. Wise friends stand against bullies. Foolish friends become bullies. Wise friends put others first. Foolish friends put themselves first.

Boys gain confidence and status by associating with boys who can do things—play sports, perform music, or otherwise challenge themselves. It is vital that we help our sons find godly companions.

It's easy to see boys acting pointlessly and assume they're not thinking. But boys think by moving. To encourage them, we need to notice what returns energy to them, making them come alive. Here's how you might talk about it with your son:

- "You can never go farther in life than the people you surround yourself with. Who are the good people you'd like to be around? How can I help make that happen?"
- "No matter what you face, there are men who have been there. Find them, listen to them, and try to be like them."

Identity: Who am I? Unleashing the Explorer

The famous explorer Ernest Shackleton was said to have recruited men for his South Pole expedition through a newspaper advertisement: "Men wanted for hazardous journey. Small wages. Bitter cold. Long months of complete darkness. Safe return doubtful. Honor and recognition in case of success." Perhaps the story is mythical, but it persists because of a core truth: men want their lives to count for something.

Boys grapple with the "Who am I?" question most successfully by going on a quest. When God created Adam, he commanded him to "subdue the earth," to bring it into his realm of understanding. The man's first act was to name the animals. To name them, Adam had to understand each animal's characteristics and how it fit into the environment God had created.

Knowing the world around them is how boys get to know themselves. Exploration helps boys understand that God designed them to act in the face of risk to bring good to their world.

Action entails risk. Boys must learn to approach the world with curiosity rather than fear, especially when they're tempted to fear other people. As J. C. Ryle put it, the fear of man is the most thankless of vices. No one admires a man who flees risk. "The world always respects those the most, who act boldly for God," he says.[15]

> For men, exploration isn't just what they do to make a living; it is what they do to make a life.

But not all exploration requires physical risk. Musical performance is a risky exploration. Writing good computer code is a risky exploration. A good life in general is an exploration. For men, exploration isn't just what they do to make a living; it is what they do to make a life. We can encourage our boys' explorations by encouraging them in wholehearted pursuits:

- "You worked really hard at that. And you got results. I knew you would!"
- "I've noticed that when you do 'X' it really grabs your attention. Let's explore that."
- "Son, I'm proud of the risk you took. You're becoming a man who doesn't flinch in the face of what's hard."
- "Son, if you're ever unsure of what to do, just ask, 'How would a good man handle this?'"
- "Look for people who do a great job and try to be like them."

There is so much to be curious about in our big, beautiful world. Take your boys on field trips everywhere you can: police stations, fire stations, factories. Visit with carpenters, welders, athletes, soldiers, landscapers, engineers, and elected officials. Learn how they pursue excellence.

As you go, encourage your son to practice the art of good questions:

- What were you interested in when you were my age?
- How did you get into this line of work?
- What do you like about your job?
- What is hard about your job?
- How do you measure good work?
- How does someone prepare to do a job like this?
- What else would you like me to know?

Belonging: Who Wants Me? Unleashing the Servant

Young men need to feel important and needed. Jesus taught his followers that you become important and needed by being a servant who lifts others up. "If anyone would be first, he must be last of all and servant of all," he said (Mark 9:35). Choosing to be a servant conquers passivity. Jordan B. Peterson says, "You are not mature until someone else matters more than you—period."[16]

Here are some discussion starters:

- "Son, as you go through your day, ask, 'What is happening and how can I help?'"
- "My heart is that you become a man of honor. That means treating people as special, doing more than what is expected, and having a good attitude." (Thank you to Scott Turansky and Joann Miller for this excellent definition.)[17]

The opposite of serving is scoffing. Scoffers jealously cope with their own insecurities by diminishing the value of others. Jesus' parable of the prodigal sons is about this. One son squandered his gifts in self-centeredness. The other squandered his gifts in self-righteousness. The self-centered son humbled himself. The self-righteous one did not. One son became a servant. The other son became a scoffer.[18]

We help our sons unleash the servant by finding areas where they can win by making meaningful contributions. Encourage them by noticing when they take steps in the right direction:

- "Son, I really appreciate the way you ask questions. It shows that you are ready to learn and serve."
- "When you encouraged that other boy, he became bolder. I'm proud of you, son."
- "I noticed you open the door for your mom. I love that. That's what real men do."

A real man is known by how he treats others. A godly man is known by how this reflects Jesus' self-sacrifice.

Purpose: Why Am I Alive? Unleashing the Warrior

In Stephen Crane's *Red Badge of Courage*, the protagonist, Henry, ran away from a battle. Ashamed, he launched furiously into the next battle. In so doing, he learned that "the world was a world for him."

Every boy is a warrior-in-training who needs to know that this world is a world for him. Some join armies. Others join orchestras. Some work in factories. Others bring healing. The "Why am I alive?" question is answered by how boys battle for truth and fight against evil and injustice in everyday life.

The "maiden in distress" is a dominant literary motif. The message to boys is, "Kill the dragon; win the girl." Most don't realize this metaphor's biblical basis. Jeremiah 9:17–18 teaches that the wailing of mourning women cracks open the heavens. Men were designed to instinctively respond to the vulnerable in a way that calms fear and restores what was lost.

Guiding Boys to Become Confident Men by Using the Core Needs

Yet the enemy of our souls causes young men to draw back, rather than press in. Our sons desperately need to understand that the enemy of their souls is an *enemy*. This is war. Every young man should claim this pledge as a badge of honor: "I want to be a man who makes good decisions, defends people, and helps things around me get better."

If we don't train our boys to become righteous warriors, they will become evil warriors. Righteous warriors respond to the pleas of the vulnerable; evil warriors turn a deaf ear to them. Righteous warriors restore; evil warriors plunder. Righteous warriors strengthen others; evil warriors weaken them. Righteous warriors have biblical character.

> **A boy doesn't have to be rough and tough or loud to be a warrior.**

When boys see themselves as righteous warriors, it shapes their all-of-life commitment to a biblical worldview. Godly manhood isn't just about seeking God above everything, but about striving to bring God *into* everything.

At the same time, we must be careful not to make the "warrior" aspect of masculinity all about being militaristic, forceful, and loud. This is a mistake that creates gender confusion. A boy doesn't have to be rough and tough or loud to be a warrior. Some warriors battle bad people. Others battle bad ideas. Still others battle cruelty, indecision, disharmony, chaos, or inefficiency. Boys can battle with ideas, position, personality, and power.

Here are three characteristics of warriors that all boys can embrace:

A warrior owns the battle space. Growing from boyhood into manhood is an all-of-life commitment. Talk with your son about pressing ahead when things get tough. Introduce him to men who have done this—Bible heroes, current heroes, and those from history. And especially ask him to observe those around him:

- "What is the difference between a man who uses people versus one who protects them?"
- "Who are men you see who push forward and overcome the odds? What's different about them?"

A warrior is full-time. Men own their faith best in their daily actions. Encourage your son in this:

- "What can you do today to honor your teacher and classmates?"
- "How can your actions today bring blessing to those around you?"

A warrior controls his power. Contrary to popular opinion, elite military units don't look for fearless people, but for people who know how to regulate their fear.[19] Masculine power under control models God's patience. Ephesians 4:31 says, "Let all bitterness and wrath and anger and clamor and slander be put away from you, along with all malice." A warrior controls his emotions, so his emotions don't control him.

- "It's easy to get mad when things don't go your way. Do you know people who aren't controlled by their 'mad'? What do they do that you can learn from?"
- "Son, real men protect and honor others even when they don't feel like it. Tell me a time when you've done this."

One of the best ways for a boy to unleash the warrior is through organized group activities such as sports, band, chess club, or debate. Through these activities, boys learn about people, make friends, set group goals, and develop resilience. Team activities help boys academically, build resistance to bad habits, work off stress, and promote mental health. Team activities give boys the opportunity to exhaust themselves in worthy pursuits. Properly framed, they prepare boys to fight for what God cares about.

Competence: What Do I Do Well? Unleashing the Husbandman

Just as God designed men to subdue the earth, he also designed them to bring growth and maturity to those around them. In Genesis 2, God placed Adam in the Garden of Eden to work it and to keep it. Boys gain competence when they know that others need them to thrive. This is where the word husband comes from. Taking care of animals is called animal husbandry because it involves helping animals thrive.

Husbandmen don't just win wives, though that is a worthy aspiration. They win trust. They learn to relate to others and build them up. This isn't easy. Boys typically have a more limited emotional vocabulary than girls. Quickly switching between tasks is hard for them.[20] Parents who've asked their son, "How was your day?" at the end of school usually get "Okay" as the answer. Answering the "How was your day?" question requires boys to switch from doing things to talking about them. It engages their entire brain, which is tired at the end of a long day. Wise parents give their sons a "half-time" after an arduous task to rest (and eat). When they're ready to talk, they'll likely volunteer more information to "What happened?" questions than "How do you feel?" questions. Here are some examples:

- "I know you had a history test today. What was it like to take it? Do you see it as a win?"
- "On the news they said the president gave a controversial speech. Is that something your teachers talked about? I'm curious how they saw it."
- "I heard that 'X, Y, or Z' video game is popular. Is that something your friends are interested in? What do they like about it? Is it something that you're interested in? What do you find interesting about it?"

A man does not naturally blossom into his calling. To become a man, a boy must conquer his boyhood. He does that by unleashing the sage, explorer, servant, warrior, and husbandman. All of this is done with the strong, guiding influence of older men who show that boys can become godly men.

Now, it's time to turn our attention to guiding girls to become godly women. Shall we get started?

DR. JEFF'S PERSPECTIVE
WHAT DADS DO

I earned my doctorate in a time when men were viewed with disdain. The traditional family was mocked, and fathers were seen as irrelevant or possibly dangerous. The famed anthropologist Margaret Mead said, "Mothers are a biological necessity; fathers are a social invention." My professors taught that and seemed to fervently believe it.

My research focused on understanding mothers' and fathers' roles in helping their children learn to communicate and think. Previous researchers treated fathers as "husbands of mothers" who played no significant role in child development. And, indeed, some of the evidence shows that fathers aren't as sensitive as mothers. They have more communication breakdowns with their kids.

But my research results revealed that father's communication styles bridge children to the outside world. Fathers help them "decenter" and connect with people who aren't like them. Children need this.

Dads, your role is crucial. You may feel that you don't understand your kids as well as their mom does, which may be true. But your time and conversations with them form an indispensable "handshake" with the real world.

DR. KATHY'S PERSPECTIVE
TALK TO YOUR DAD

It's not always easy for girls to understand men or for men to understand girls, but we've got to keep trying—especially in our families.

Each summer, the company my dad worked for hired their employees' children who were in college. I jumped at the job and drove to and from work for three summers with my dad. During this season, I was most grateful for one-on-one time with my dad, not the job or money I earned.

I got to know my dad better, and I understood him more. I no longer saw him as quiet and too serious; I saw him as wise and thoughtful. I recognized his heart for me, my brother, and my mom; I no longer regretted that he didn't emote much. I saw his quiet as a good quality, not evidence that he didn't care. I wanted him to know me better, and I also discovered he knew and understood me better than I thought he did.

I discovered why my dad liked what he did and why he was good at it. I learned to honor him as our provider and protector in a much deeper way. I still remember how I felt when others talked about and praised my dad. If you ask me, I can still recall a tremendous victory my dad orchestrated.

My dad grew before my eyes. These rides were not about the child being seen, which is usually the case, and what I thought I needed. They were about the child seeing the dad. That's what I needed. Do you still need this? See your dad. Or, are you a dad reading, and you want your daughter to know you? See your daughter. Talk and listen; it will be good for you both.

Want more strategies for helping boys become confident men? Download the Chapter Six resource, "The 8 Great Smarts for Boys," at genderconfidentkids.com.

CHAPTER 7

GUIDING GIRLS TO BECOME CONFIDENT WOMEN BY USING THE EIGHT SMARTS

We start this chapter with a settled conviction: gender confidence rises on the shoulders of identity confidence. When a teenage girl can name how God wired her and why that wiring matters, she stands steady in her own skin.

This chapter is written differently from the rest of the book, on purpose. We're inviting you into Wayne and Nancy Stender's living room, and Nancy's dorm hallway, where she serves as a dorm mom and mentor to high school girls at Hillcrest Academy. Wayne and Nancy partner with Kathy to inspire parents with their ministry, Celebrate Kids. We asked them to write this chapter because they've ministered to teen girls to build identity confidence for over 20 years. They have a lot of insight here, and we want to show you how identity confidence grows to form gender confidence.

Pour something warm, settle into a chair, and let's build the kind of confidence that can't be shaken. Wayne and Nancy, you've got the floor.

Wayne knew something was off the instant his daughter slid through the front door. Her backpack hit the floor with a thud, and after a probing, "How are you," she offered the quick kind of "fine" that only parents translate as *anything but fine*. Seconds later, she was in her room, door closed. Thirty minutes later, having given the silence time to breathe, Wayne knocked softly.

As the door slowly opened, Wayne discovered a universe on the floor. His girl was sprawled out on the carpet, sketching silver-winged heroes, whole worlds swirling across the carpet. His daughter sat up, her back against the bedpost, picture-smart fingers calling creatures to life. He paused and named what he saw: the shading on the cloaks was realistic, and the way the maiden's hair billowed looked like the artist was blowing on the picture. With every affirmation, her pencil moved faster, a quiet rhythm of color and feeling. Yet, the fog behind her eyes never lifted.

Wayne nudged, "Tell me about today."

A few gentle loops of conversation finally led to the question that mattered: "Do you feel like you relate well to your friends?"

The pencil stopped moving as Wayne's daughter whispered, "No."

Most boys may find their identity in competence, what they can do. But in our experience, girls make sense of *who* they are by *where* they belong. When belonging fractures, every other layer of identity trembles: security, identity, purpose, competence. In Chapter Three, we read about the five core needs, and we believe each one fuels identity confidence, which in turn leads to gender confidence. When even one need is starved, identity feels negotiable; when all five are nourished, a girl stands rooted in who God designed her to be.

Wayne didn't launch a lecture. He settled on the floor, eye level, unhurried, and let presence preach safety. Security always speaks first: *You're safe with me.*

Then he asked, "Do you want to know how people discover who they are?"

She nodded, tears dotting the paper below.

Wayne told stories of each of his eight kids, eight studies in Kathy's *8 Great Smarts*.[1] (If you're unfamiliar with the book's framework, that's okay. Wayne will explain it in the next few pages.) His daughter's youngest brother is body smart, forever dribbling basketballs and consistently getting talked to at school. A smirk flung across his daughter's face. Her closest brother is logic smart, thrilled by riddles at breakfast and history stories at night. Wayne's daughter nodded. With every anecdote about every sibling, his daughter's shoulders eased: the differences weren't defects; they were design.

Finally, Wayne turned the spotlight on her: "You're self smart and picture smart. You feel deeply and imagine vividly. That's why math problems feel like prison bars; they're too straight for the way your mind dances. But it's also why you're the first one to see beauty where others see chaos."

> **When girls are seen in their smarts and secure in their core needs, identity confidence stops feeling like a riddle and starts feeling like a slow inhale of cool mountain air.**

Her lip trembled, this time with relief. Someone had decoded her. Identity clicked into place: *I'm not weird; I'm brilliantly wired.*

When girls are *seen* in their smarts and *secure* in their core needs, identity confidence stops feeling like a riddle and starts feeling like a slow inhale of cool mountain air: natural, God-breathed, steady. Wayne's daughter still draws cloaked maidens, but now their eyes shine with something new: a quiet certainty that the Artist who chose his canvas knew precisely what he was doing.

We need to give girls time to build their identity and realize who they are. They need time because our hurry-up culture expects them to have immediate answers about nearly everything, and the pressure is unbearable.

Tools like Alexa, Siri, and ChatGPT are the information equivalent of instant coffee: unrefined and utterly lacking in nuance. They offer quick-fix answers to questions that would mean so much more if girls discovered them rather than flipping to the last page to see how things turned out.

In this chapter, we'd like to show how girls' identities flower through how their core needs are met and as they have time to reflect on and grow confident in their natural smarts. As parents, it's crucial that we approach our young girls with grace, patience, and kindness. This will allow them to form strong identities amidst cultural pressure while providing the proper framework for them to build confidence.

BUILDING THE PYRAMID OF CONFIDENCE BY MEETING CORE NEEDS

We recommend that you become familiar with how identity is cultivated for flourishing through the meeting of core needs, as we talked about in Chapter Three. Learning how to help our children have their core needs met through God is vital to identity formation.

Picture the core-needs pyramid as a five-step ascent:

- *Security* is the ground floor; build it by taking 10 phone-free minutes of calm eye contact and the steady promise, "Nothing you say will drive me away."

Guiding Girls to Become Confident Women by Using the Eight Smarts

- On that footing, *Identity* forms the second tier when parents name God's wiring, "Your picture-smart eye isn't weird; it's wired." Recording each tiny triumph in a family strength journal is a sacred liturgy that secures this stage.
- Confidence in who she is opens the door to *Belonging*: family projects that rely on every smart say, "You fit here."
- Next comes *Purpose*, the choice to use gifts for service. Art turned into cards for shut-ins, beats mixed for nursery lullabies, story after story proving talent is a mission, not a hobby.
- At the summit stands *Competence*, visible progress affirmed by tools that match her learning style and micro-challenges just beyond yesterday's reach; each win whispering, "You're not just gifted; you're growing," and the whole structure stands firm enough to bear lifelong gender confidence.

When *security* is in place, a child is confident enough to risk asking *identity* questions.

When *identity* feels solid, *belonging* becomes possible.

Belonging opens the door to *purpose*, and repeated purpose wins *competence*.

Loop through the pyramid often, especially in the pre-teen and teen years, when your girl is tempted to change who she is to fit in. Your steady presence, specific praise, and purposeful invitations give daughters (and sons) the sturdy internal strength to answer the cultural confusion around gender with calm, biblically-grounded confidence: *"I know whose I am, so I know who I am."*

THE 8 GREAT SMARTS—WHY THEY MATTER FOR YOUR DAUGHTER'S IDENTITY AND HER GENDER CONFIDENCE

When girls build identity confidence, it reinforces how they're wired for the world. Sadly, society still sorts strengths into blue and pink boxes.

Girls who are word-lovers are called "chatty" and "bossy." Logic-smart girls are told they're "cold" and "insensitive." Athletic girls are "tomboys" if they want to play with the guys. Those who think in pictures and chase a profession with their talents may want to be an architect, but are told they "think like a man." One Summit Ministries student told Jeff, "As soon as I announced in my class that I wanted to be an engineer, I was told, 'You must be a boy in a girl's body.'"

If your daughter keeps hearing these messages, it's natural to jump from "my talents don't fit me" to "my gender is wrong for who I am." She may want to grow in her giftings, but can hesitate because she doesn't want to think her gender is wrong and she definitely doesn't want others to think that either. She won't have identity confidence or gender confidence and could also deny her interests and abilities.

> When girls build identity confidence, it reinforces how they're wired for the world.

Some girls are **word smart**; their identity is built in storytelling or naming every Disney or Pokémon character with ridiculous accuracy. Others are **logic smart,** where asking "Why?" 75 times a day builds mental systems. Some **picture-smart** girls doodle life's questions in the margins of math homework. Some **music-smart** girls hear melodies in moments and sense God's whisper between notes. **Body-smart** girls navigate the world intuitively, learning through motion, rhythm, and touch. **Nature-smart** girls collect rocks and notice clouds while the rest of us barely see the sky.

Guiding Girls to Become Confident Women by Using the Eight Smarts

People-smart girls know how you feel before you say a word, and **self-smart** girls think deeply and won't answer a question until they *really* know what they believe.

Psychology proves these eight smarts.[2] They are how we relate to the world, and as the girls in our lives mature to women, they will relate to the world through these intelligences. Kathy's book *8 Great Smarts*[3] opens intelligence and proves every girl is smart. However, as girls grow up, be careful and alert because the world stereotypes their giftings.

Society might tell them the wiring is right, but the packaging is wrong. However, imagotype thinking based on how God made them transcends stereotypes, so as girls develop full confidence in God, they strengthen their identity confidence, which in turn fosters gender confidence. Then they can navigate the world with the calm assurance that this is how it is supposed to be.

Sometimes our girls know what they're good at. But just as Zina Garrison helped mentor tennis champion Serena Williams to greatness, our girls need us to move from caretaker to coach to awaken and inspire growth in who they are. Let's dive into these smarts, some of the stereotypes, and how we can reinforce an imagotype confidence that leads to competence and gender security.

Word-Smart Girls Relate with Words

Picture your daughter volleying ideas across the dinner table. She's quick and clever, commanding the table, but a whisper hisses in her ear: *Real debaters wear power suits and ties.* That lie has cousins. Class clowns? Always guys. Courtroom sharks? Men in tailored suits. Word-smart girls wrestle with feelings that their verbal brilliance is masculine, and they often stay quiet, wondering if they're out of place or in the wrong body.

Pull up a chair and really hear her by chasing new vocabulary down etymology rabbit holes so she sees language as a discovery, not as a way of showing off. Hand her a public microphone, for the family slideshow or Sunday announcements.

> Teach your daughter she's not simply clever, but crafted.

When you consistently listen, platform, shape, and celebrate her language gift, your daughter stops wondering whether she's "too much." Instead, she hears a louder truth: *I am perfectly wired, profoundly female, and equipped to build, heal, and guide with every sentence I speak.* That's identity confidence feeding gender confidence, spoken into being, one purposeful word at a time.

Teach your daughter she's not simply clever, but crafted. Her words translate truth. God laced her voice with power to light and lead to life. When she unveils the right word at the right time it's more than talent, it's testimony. She is wholly whole echoing the Author who spoke and created light, and gives her the gift to speak his words uniting his story to others.

Logic-Smart Girls Relate with Questions

Your daughter opens the dishwasher, scans the jumble of plates, and, before you can blink, re-stacks everything into perfect rows to maximize water efficiency. She recites multiplication facts like poetry. She loves brain-teaser podcasts and, yes, she corrects the teacher's math (occasionally). A quiet doubt follows her triumphs: *Girls who think like this are masculine . . . insensitive . . . maybe my gifts make me "manly."*

Rewrite that internal script. Start by expanding her gallery of heroes: Lady Wisdom from Proverbs,[4] standing in the street, urging passersby to reason, or Lydia[5] negotiating contracts for purple dye. Slip those stories into bedtime, car rides, and science homework margins.

Next, coach her to see logic as love in action. Hand her the family grocery budget and a mission: shave off 10 dollars while adding an item for the food pantry. Watch her eyes light up as data becomes generosity.

Name what you see: "Your pattern-brain doesn't cancel your empathy; it protects it. God created you to spot problems *and* the people hidden inside them."

Reason with her that she isn't asking "why" in an aimless refrain. God wired her mind to connect the dots that no one sees and to build bridges where others hit walls. Every question she asks reveals a pattern to solve. This is a signpost that she's wholly whole in deciphering mysteries in the world. She's purposely crafted by the God who set gravity to guard the galaxies and placed her to understand how, why, and join him in this creative endeavor.

Picture-Smart Girls Relate with Visuals and Colors

Your daughter can turn an empty margin into a universe. Dragons spiral up math worksheets, and color palettes bloom inside every cereal box she opens. Still, a faint worry shadows the charcoal dust on her fingertips: *I hope no one sees this. Boys are the ones who get distracted. Doodling is "cute," not serious. Maybe I'm just a hyperactive boy in the wrong body.*

Time to redraw the framework. Begin by stocking her mental gallery with women who sculpted history: Bezalel's spirit-filled craftsmanship[6] has a New Testament sister in Tabitha,[7] who stitched beauty into generosity. Help her test drive her talent in service: commission her to redesign the family chore chart or paint the backdrop for Vacation Bible School. Watch confidence rise when her vision guides real traffic flow or lifts kids' eyes to Jesus. Ask her to illustrate Sunday's sermon, then talk through what those visuals make people *feel*. Encourage a sketch journal where she processes disappointments in color and celebrates wins in silhouette, translating emotion into image instead of bottling it.

Name the truth out loud: "Your restless eye for beauty isn't fluff; it's engineering heaven's hope into earth's chaos. God wired you to see what others miss and invite them inside." Once that affirmation takes root, blue-and-pink stereotypes fade like pencil guidelines beneath finished art, and she stands wholly whole, every stroke an echo of the Creator who painted first light across the void.

Music-Smart Girls Relate with Sounds, Rhythms, and Melodies

Your daughter hears melody in the dishwasher's rhythm and finds harmonies in the rain gutter's drip. Yet an uneasy refrain plays in the background: *Real producers are guys; girls just sing the pretty part. Maybe I'm wired wrong for the tech side.*

Stock her mental playlist with women who moved nations by moving sound: Miriam shaking a tambourine after the Red Sea[8] is a good start. Then, have her splice audio for Grandma's video tribute. Watch her confidence swell when the screeching feedback disappears because *she* caught the rogue frequency.

Say it clearly: "Your ear isn't just nice; it's necessary. God designed you to tune chaos into harmony and let people hear hope." When that truth hits her headphones, the stereotype fades to static, and she stands wholly whole, every beat an echo of the Creator who sang the morning stars into chorus.[9]

Body-Smart Girls Relate with Movement, Action, and Touch

Your daughter moves like sunrise: fast, sure, irrepressible. She vaults from the couch, dribbles anything round, turns cartwheels while brainstorming history facts, and feels most herself when muscles sing and lungs burn. Yet a nagging voice follows every grass stain: *Girls who don't mind sweating are tomboys; maybe you'd fit better on the other team.*

Unleash her gift in service: assign her to design the relay course for church picnic games, heft boxes for the food bank drive, or choreograph a

Guiding Girls to Become Confident Women by Using the Eight Smarts

worship dance that tells the Creation story. Applaud new personal records in races and cleaner cartwheels, then double the applause when she pauses mid-scrimmage to help a fallen opponent or coaches a shy classmate over the climbing wall.

All of this stamps the truth on her heart: "Your strength isn't a glitch; it's a gift. God fashioned your muscles to shield, build, and celebrate life, all while remaining fully, gloriously female." Once that affirmation sinks to the marrow, labels like "tomboy" lose traction, and she stands wholly whole, every sprint an echo of the Savior who walked on water and still calls daughters to run their race.

Nature-Smart Girls Relate in Nature and Think in Patterns

Your daughter can read the sky like a diary. She smells rain an hour before the first drop, tracks ants the way others track TikTok trends, and pockets acorns "just in case." Yet every muddy sneaker carries a taunt: *Girls who like dirt must be boyish.*

Shift the forecast by filling her imagination with women who healed the world through creation care: Hagar spotting a lifesaving well in the desert[10] and shepherd-girl Rachel managing water for life and care.[11]

Explore science and wonder: how worm castings nourish the soil *and* remind us that God recycles broken things; how migrating geese serve as models for faith communities on the move. Hand her a field notebook for sketches, weather stats, and prayers of thanks, and celebrate each new species ID as loudly as any A grade. Anchor the truth: "You're not weird for loving dirt; you're wired to echo the first job God gave humanity, cultivate and keep his masterpiece."[12]

Once that affirmation sinks deeper than tree roots, the "mud-means-male" myth washes away, and she stands wholly whole, every observation an echo of the Creator who called the earth good and asked his daughters to explore it.

People-Smart Girls Relate with People

Your daughter can read a room the way sailors read stars, spotting a wobble in her friend's smile, rearranging chairs so Mr. Lee's bad knee gets the aisle, and defusing sibling quarrels with a joke before anyone else senses tension. But each socially tuned victory carries a jab: *Girls this "feely-aware" are drama queens—or worse, manipulative.*

Time to flip the script. Fill her story bank with women whose relational radar changed history: Esther hosting two dinners that unmasked genocide plans[13] and Priscilla guiding Apollos' theology in living-room conversation.[14] Unlock her gift in real service: appoint her as "connection captain" for the youth retreat icebreakers. Afterward, debrief like a coach after a game: What body-language cues tipped her off? Which question opened hearts? Help her see that God designed her to spot hidden hurts and to weave people together, precisely as a *daughter* after His own heart.

When that truth settles, the drama-queen label dissolves, and she stands wholly whole, every smile salvaged an echo of the Shepherd who leaves ninety-nine to find the one.[15]

Self-Smart Girls Relate with Reflection, Quiet, and Peace

Your daughter keeps a fortress of silence the way others keep playlists, retreating to the porch swing with a journal and tea, charting emotions in color codes known only to her and God. Yet each reflective pause comes with an accusation: *Quiet girls are moody, over-dramatic, or self-absorbed—maybe even too sensitive to be strong.* Culture nudges the lie with memes ridiculing "over-thinkers," movie heroes who act first and feel later, and friends who call her room "the cave." Time to rewrite these stories.

Stock her inner library with women whose solitude steered nations: Hannah pouring out unspoken prayers,[16] Mary "pondering all these things" into incarnation history.[17] Jesus himself slipped away before dawn to connect with his Father before saying a word.[18] Have your self-smart daughter design a family reflection ritual that uses candles, silence, and a well-placed question; let her craft reflective prompts for the youth retreat; ask her to mentor a younger sibling in keeping a feelings journal. Debrief like detectives: What patterns surfaced? Which question unlocked gratitude?

At every turn, speak this headline: "Your deep dive isn't drama; it's discernment. God wired your inner radar to chart safe passage for yourself and others, and that gift is fully, gloriously feminine." When that truth settles beneath the quiet, the moody-girl myth evaporates, and she stands wholly whole; every journal page an echo of the Savior who knew the crowd's thoughts[19] because he first listened to the Father in secret.[20]

OUR JOB AS PARENTS: HOLD THE LANTERN WHILE SHE EXPLORES

When a girl can trace every smart in her wiring, she sees that logic orders chaos, art splashes hope, and strength lifts the weary back to the God who planted it there. The mirror stops feeling like a verdict and starts feeling like a commission.

> Our task as parents is simply to hold the lantern while she discovers how her gifts reflect God's character and extend his Gospel.

She hears the core needs questions: *Who can I trust? Who am I? Who wants me? Why am I alive? What do I do well?* and finds Jesus answering each one with scarred hands and a steady "I AM." Identity settles, competence blooms, and gender confidence rises naturally from the soil of that settled love; being female is no longer a glitch to correct but a glory to steward.

Our task as parents is simply to hold the lantern while she discovers how her gifts reflect God's character and extend his Gospel. Once she sees that her very design participates in heaven's story, nothing in culture can convince her otherwise.

And that kind of girl, confident in how her Creator made her, can instinctively know how to harmonize with others for the good of the world. It's true for boys as well, and men and women. Once we learn to rise above cultural stereotypes with imagotypes based on who we are as image-bearers of God, we can see that gender is at the heart of God's beautiful plan for humanity itself.

Want more strategies for helping girls become confident women? Download the Chapter Seven resource, "Meeting the Core Needs of Girls," at genderconfidentkids.com.

CHAPTER 8

GUIDING BOYS AND GIRLS, MEN AND WOMEN TO HARMONIZE—WE NEED EACH OTHER

Our friend and fellow Summit Ministries speaker, Alycia Wood, is a highly educated woman and gifted communicator. *And* she played hockey for over 20 years. Talk about breaking down stereotypes!

As an adult, Alycia began to understand that some male/female differences are brain deep, causing men and women to play hockey differently even when they play together. For a time, Alycia competed in a co-ed hockey league. "I just remember playing with the guys and thinking, 'What are you doing? Why did you pass there?' I was so confused. And then I went to play on the all-girls team that I was part of, and I knew exactly where I needed to go and what my teammates were doing. It was so interesting. I can't read the men the same way I can read the women. I know how the women think."[1]

Volumes of research verify Alycia's observation. Leonard Sax, a medical doctor and PhD psychologist, acknowledges many similarities between how boys and girls learn, interact, and play. And yet, he insists, "human nature is gendered to the core."[2] Sax writes, "[Girls labeled as tomboys] have more in common with very feminine girls than they have with boys, at least when it comes to how they see the world."[3]

In the first draft of this book, we included a raft of studies about the biological differences between boys and girls. But as we discussed how to use all this data, our team became concerned that if a girl reads about typical female attributes and says, "I don't identify with that at all," she might begin thinking she was born in the wrong body. And vice versa for boys. Therefore, we only wove in enough to make some key points about how the two types of humans—male and female—harmonize. Our overriding goal in this chapter is to rise above cultural stereotypes by marveling at the wisdom of God's imagotypes.

> Cultural stereotypes have made it difficult to talk about how boys and girls have been made differently in God's image.

Cultural stereotypes have made it difficult to talk about how boys and girls have been made differently in God's image. As we discussed how to handle the issue, Jeff reflected on his life experience. Both his brothers are musicians with extraordinary emotional intelligence, something that cultural stereotypes say is a feminine trait. Would they be told today that they are girls stuck in boys' bodies? One of Jeff's daughters is a helicopter pilot. Would she be told that she excels in a male-dominated field because she is really a boy?

When we focus on either reinforcing or trying to tear down cultural stereotypes about gender, we risk freezing these differences and interpreting them in a way that plants seeds of doubt about God's design.

How do we handle this? Let us state the obvious. Males and females both have skeletons, brains, hearts, digestive systems, and circulatory systems. We're far more alike than we are different when it comes to our organ systems.

And yet, differences exist—thousands of them. Whether our talking about them plays into cultural stereotypes or rises above them depends on how we interpret them with wisdom.

That's why the last two chapters were about helping boys and girls become confident in their gender by rising above culturally-based stereotypes. Instead, we focus on what we think of as biblically-based imagotypes that reflect the fact that we humans are made in God's image.

Our culture has trained us to think that male and female differences have moral content, that one or the other is "superior," and that everyone would be better off if males were more like females, or vice versa. This often leads to envy. Girls might say, "If I were a boy, I wouldn't be weak and easy to hurt." Boys might say, "If I knew how to read emotions better, I wouldn't feel so out of place."

But differences are just differences, not moral categories. We would all be a lot better off if we understood this. The high school boys we work with often ask, "Why are girls so complicated?" In separate conversations, high school girls ask, "Why are boys so unpredictable?" Those who are married sometimes wonder, in frustration, whether their marriage would be better if their spouse thought and acted more like they do. Male and female co-workers find themselves unnecessarily at odds as well. You have probably noticed young children who are aware of differences and puzzled by them, too.

And to make things even more complicated, a "non-binary" mindset is rising that says that males and females are interchangeable, or that the differences between them are irrelevant. If you've ever heard a transgender activist try to grapple with the question, "What is a woman?" you've encountered a non-binary mindset. (If you are curious about *why* they find that question so hard, check out the endnote.)[4]

So, instead of offering a comprehensive list of male/female differences, we'd like to share three inspiring examples of how those differences harmonize together to glorify God and inspire purposeful living. Differences aren't irrelevant. Males and females aren't interchangeable. We are designed to work together, boys and girls, men and women, to honor God and maintain a flourishing society.

Harmony comes from the Greek word *harmonía*, meaning to be in synch. Its opposite is dissonance. Both musical terms describe the pleasing sound when notes work together, or the noise generated when they don't.

Jeff likes to think about the analogy of superpowers. Comic book superheroes in Marvel's Avengers or DC's Justice League find themselves at each other's throats, quarreling and competing, until they are confronted by a common enemy that cannot be defeated unless they work together.

> Boys and girls, men and women, have been given different superpowers.

Boys and girls, men and women, have been given different superpowers. Will we use them to fight for dominance in an epic "battle of the sexes," or will we combine our forces to fight evil and injustice and bring blessing to the world?

Here are three examples of the way God designed males and females to harmonize:

Example #1: Males and Females Need Each Other to Grow in Character

One woman told us that as a teen, her glasses, braces, and frizzy hair made her feel out of sorts as a girl. A wise female mentor told her, "Someday you'll get contacts, lose the braces, and figure out what to do with your hair. But what you have cultivated during this time of your life—your character—*that's* forever."

Character rarely forms in solitude. Boys and girls, men and women, need each other to be sharpened and grow in character. God has graciously given us choice in many things and withheld choice in others. We can't choose our physical size, nationality, parentage, or siblings. We can't control the times into which we were born. We can't choose our gender.

But if we accept that males and females are different, and that this difference is God-inspired, we can honor and communicate about those differences. Acknowledging differences creates a level of respect that is good for the world. Respect is foundational to good character.

Our Jewish friends have something to teach us about honoring male and female differences. Jewish families celebrate the harmonious differences of men and women every week on Shabbat, as husbands sing a portion of Proverbs 31 to their wives to celebrate their ingenuity, hard work, and moral excellence.

Example #2: Males and Females Need Each Other to Accurately See the World

When his children were little, Jeff gave them colored pencils and paper to help them sit still in church. Invariably, the girls used all the colors to draw their home, family, flowers, and abstract designs. The boys only needed black and red: black to draw the tanks and airplanes, and red to draw the blood squirting out of those who were shot.

It's been said, as a generalization, that girls draw nouns and boys draw verbs. Some of the biological differences between boys and girls might help explain why this is often true. Dr. Leonard Sax explains that girls have a preponderance of parvocellular cells (P-cells) in their eyes. P-cells compile information about texture and color. Boys have a preponderance of magnocellular cells (M-cells) in their eyes. M-cells are motion detectors, compiling information about movement and direction.[5] These different types of retinal cells send information to different parts of the brain.

Girls and boys both have M-cells and P-cells. But knowing that they aren't evenly distributed among boys and girls helps us understand harmony. The fullest picture of life incorporates color, texture, movement, and direction. Isn't it fascinating that God designed boys and girls, men and women, to need each other to see things as they really are?

> But with harmony as our goal, we can respect and celebrate the differences.

Over time, many such differences have been observed to be generally true of boys and girls. Girls have more sensitive hearing than boys. Girls are 10 times as distracted by noise as boys. Boys take more risks, and for different reasons than most girls express. Girls in general find it easier to sit still in class. Girls sometimes fight, but boys fight 20 times more. In the workplace, men and women have most goals in common, but dozens of studies show that women's workplace values are more likely to include communication and collaboration, while men's workplace values generally gravitate toward pay, benefits, and status.[6]

If our culture teaches us to view any of these differences as right or wrong, males and females will always find themselves at odds. But with harmony as our goal, we can respect and celebrate the differences.

Example #3: Males and Females Need Each Other to Respond Effectively to Stress

Among mammals, male and female bodies respond differently to stress.[7] It does us no good to refuse to acknowledge this, especially for those who are trying to help males or females cope with stress-related anxiety or disease. A one-size solution doesn't fit all. But if we think of males and females working together, we can see that their stress-coping mechanisms harmonize to create a stronger response than either males or females would possess in isolation.

> Boys and girls, men and women, are different. God made them that way.

This goes back to God's design. Girls are more likely to process stimuli through the prefrontal cortex (by thinking), and boys through the amygdala (by acting). A typical male may face threats by instinctively moving into action, whereas a typical female might focus more on interpreting and remembering facial expressions and assessing the feelings involved.[8]

Both are needed for effective conflict resolution. If you aren't instinctively willing to act, your problems pile up. But if you don't accurately perceive what is happening, you can make your problems worse. Overthinking can be bad. Overreacting can be bad. A proper amount of each is needed. God designed males and females to bring that balance.

WISDOM: GOD'S GIFT TO HELP US HARMONIZE

Gender issues are complex. But with a biblical worldview, we've been given a way to unlock harmony. It's called wisdom. Wisdom transforms *information* into *formation*. From the time they're young, we can help our sons and daughters grasp that it honors God's design to work together, respect our differences, and demonstrate harmony to the world.

Wisdom alerts us to the danger of enshrining cultural stereotypes. But it also tells us that it is unwise to react so strongly against them that we ignore the insights of the ages. Social philosopher Michael Gurian quotes an African proverb relating to the childbearing aspect of women's design: "A girl can know that life will grow right beneath her heart—a boy cannot. He knows he will have to grow life with his hands."[9]

Boys and girls, men and women, are different. God made them that way. Confidence in their gender will result in a harmony that is good for the world. This is true while they are young and whether they remain single or marry when they are grown.

You might be wondering: "What do we do with this information? How does it make a difference?" The answer is that it is foundational to discovering how boys and girls, men and women, can stand for God's truth in a culture that seems intent on either denying it or twisting it. That's what we'll talk about—and illustrate—next.

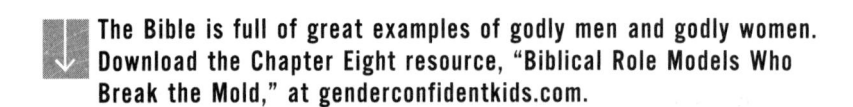

> **The Bible is full of great examples of godly men and godly women. Download the Chapter Eight resource, "Biblical Role Models Who Break the Mold," at genderconfidentkids.com.**

CHAPTER 9

PREPARING BOYS AND GIRLS AND YOU TO STAND FOR TRUTH—THREE TESTED STRATEGIES

Most people believe there are two genders, male and female. Yet many who reject this truth occupy positions of power in human resources, politics, and education. Short of denying the Bible and ignoring human biology, there is little you can say or do to win them over, even if you're polite.

One Summit Ministries graduate, a gracious, mild-mannered medical student, asked a clarifying question about transgenderism in class. The professor took offense and placed a disciplinary notice in the student's file, which could complicate the student's opportunities for advanced training or licensure. There is no appeal. All this happened because the professor interpreted his question as a disagreement with so-called gender-affirming care.

This isn't an isolated incident. Nearly every student we ask about it says that holding to a biblical understanding of gender has caused tension in their personal relationships, job, or school. They aren't looking for trouble. They don't relish being "that person" who "doesn't get it." We imagine you don't either. But we want you and your children to be ready. How will you talk about gender confidence with children? Or help your child have those conversations with peers?

In this chapter, we'll equip you to take a stand God's way and help your child do the same. This is Plan A. There is no Plan B. We'll offer specific "how to say it" suggestions. As you read, you might think, "I wish I would have known this 5 years ago!" Please set aside any feelings of regret or shame. What we do going forward is what matters.

In our work with Gen Z young adults, we've learned three steps that help them stand for truth: *acknowledge complexity*, *invite conversation*, and *compose a strategy* for tricky situations. These will work for all ages, including you.

STEP #1: ACKNOWLEDGE COMPLEXITY: GENDER CONFUSION AND THE LOSS OF FAITH

Sexuality has become such a point of tension that one-third of young adults who disengaged from their faith say that the church's negative treatment of lesbian and gay people is one of the main reasons they left.[1]

If people struggling with their gender or sexuality were bullied at church, that's inexcusable. But that doesn't seem to be what's happening.

Preparing Boys and Girls and You to Stand for Truth—Three Tested Strategies

Half of LGBTQ people say they are religious, and about 20% attend church at least once a month.[2] That percentage is slightly less than American church attendance in general, but nearly identical to the attendance of Gen Z as a whole.[3] And churches that openly affirm LGBTQ are shrinking, not growing. So, what is going on?

> Jesus wants to transform every part of us, including our understanding of our gender and our sexuality.

We sense that young adults aren't reacting negatively to the Bible's teaching about gender. Honestly, they aren't that familiar with it, and when we bring it up, they're always fascinated. We think they're reacting against the *way* churches address difficult issues, being insensitive about gender or not talking about it at all.

Jesus wants to transform every part of us, including our understanding of our gender and our sexuality. If churches ignore or dismiss complex issues that keep people from Jesus, Gen Zers will check out, as will many others.

We won't kid you. The risk of young people abandoning their childhood faith is shockingly high. Every year, we meet young adults who grew up in church, went to college (even Christian colleges), and embraced an ungodly worldview, which they subsequently justified by developing an arrogant attitude toward those they saw as "unenlightened."

But this kind of walking away is not inevitable. When we encounter twentysomethings who remain faithful to the Lord, we often ask, "What is your church experience like?" Three themes emerge. First, their church intentionally addresses difficult topics with love and logic. Second, older adults in their church invest in helping younger adults be successful. Third, their church environment is authentic, not superficial.

Read that list again. Shouldn't these three themes permeate our homes, not just our churches? How can we make that happen?

HOW TO SAY IT

- "Transgenderism has become a complicated issue and people have strong feelings about it. How should we go about talking about issues like this?"
- "I must admit that I haven't thought as much about gender identity as I should have. Can we explore it together?"
- "I realize that you not only need answers, but answers that help you hold your head high when you're interacting with those around you."
- "Let's pray for wisdom about how to talk about emotionally charged issues."

STEP #2: INVITE CONVERSATION: STANDING FOR TRUTH THE JESUS WAY

A biblical worldview of truth doesn't just hold to logical arguments. It proclaims that truth is found in a person, Jesus. Jesus was always truthful and always relational. To be like Jesus, we must boldly and compassionately share truth and disagree without being disagreeable. This is especially true in conversations about gender identity.

It's okay to play dumb. Make your operative phrase, "Can you help me understand?" For example, here's how it might sound in relation to four types of questions our Summit Ministries' faculty teach:

- **"What do you mean?"** "Can you help me understand what you mean when you say that gender is each person's choice?"
- **"How did you arrive at that conclusion?"** "Can you help me understand what happened to your friends that caused them to see themselves as transgender?"

Preparing Boys and Girls and You to Stand for Truth–Three Tested Strategies

- **"How do you know that?"** "Can you help me understand why you think there is a difference between biological sex and gender? Is this based on facts or is it an opinion that you've heard?"
- **"What happens if you're wrong?"** "Can you help me understand why your friends think it helps to believe they were born in the wrong body? What if it turns out to be something deeper that we missed because we weren't thinking clearly about it?"

Adults like conversing with those who are curious, who seem to understand, and who envision a brighter future. Children are no different. Here are some ways to ask questions about gender that display curiosity, understanding, and vision:

"I'M CURIOUS."

- "How are you feeling about all this talk of switching genders? Is this something your coaches talk about? Your friends? What do they say?"
- "How should we respond to people who are struggling? Do we have to agree with everything they say to help them?"
- "I know our friends affect us a lot. How would you say your friends are doing emotionally? Are they feeling anxious? Are some feeling sad for no reason? Is it rubbing off on you at all?"

"I UNDERSTAND."

- "I can't really relate to the specific situation of a girl who wants to be seen as a boy, but I definitely remember times as a kid when I felt confused and wondered if there was something wrong with me."

- "When I was a kid, I remember feeling that the adults in my life didn't understand me. What do you wish adults knew about you and your friends?"
- "I remember how awkward it is to talk about some topics. Is talking about transgenderism awkward? What do you think makes it so hard?"

"I ENVISION."

- "There are times in life where we feel uncomfortable in our bodies. I see you as the kind of person who trusts God with your doubts and tries to do what is right, not just get rid of the uncomfortable feelings."
- "A lot of people are confused and don't know where to turn. One thing I have never regretted is getting to know God through the Bible."
- "When you're grown up, how would you want to look back on this situation and how you handled it?"

STEP #3: COMPOSE A STRATEGY: TRUSTING GOD WHEN THINGS GET TOUGH

Children and young adults do not receive support in their schools and jobs for maintaining a biblical worldview. Like all of us, they must be constantly vigilant to avoid being taken captive. They need reliable sources of truth—people, podcasts, books, and other resources to help them grow. They need to stay close to God through prayer, Bible study, worship, fellowship with other believers, and engagement at a biblically faithful church.

We can be strong for our kids and give them the courage to be strong. Our friend Kendall Qualls, a business leader whose ministry *TakeCharge* lifts young men and women out of a poverty mindset, told us on a podcast that his constant refrain to his children was, "The world is full of problem identifiers but very few problem solvers. Be problem solvers."[4] We want you and your children to be solution focused. This mindset makes all the difference!

In this section, we'll explore very specific ways to be solution-focused problem solvers and encourage our children to do the same.

Become Assured of God's Presence

Don't you love it when movies end "happily ever after"? But from God's perspective, there's so much more to living than the ending! Reflect on Jewish author Dennis Prager's comment on Israel's wilderness journey: "Our lives are lived mostly in the long and ordinary stretches of wilderness, not in the revelations, epiphanies, and dramatic moments of Exodus."[5] We and our children can expect times in the wilderness. We will suffer.

Suffering is often caused by recognizing that something important has been lost. What does your worldview say about relentless suffering? To medicate? To deny it? To blame others? These are unwise and unhealthy views.

The Bible's approach to suffering is not to medicate, deny, or blame. Rather, it shows how Jesus is making all things new. His sacrifice on the cross has broken the power of evil. At the same time, God identifies with us in our suffering. We're never alone or forsaken.[6] Many authors in Scripture questioned God, "Why are you silent in suffering?" God doesn't mind. Why? Because he is *right there*. In music, silence sequences the notes to make melody possible. A musical piece is a conversation; without strategically placed silence, the conversation would be jumbled. God's silence is not absence. It is an intense presence.

HOW TO SAY IT

- "I know it feels lonely to stand for what is right. You're going to make it through, and you will be so much more patient. You will have compassion for people and wisdom to share. And you will know that God will never leave you or forsake you."[7]

Learn to be Comfortable Being Uncomfortable

Many parents say happiness is their highest goal for their children. Perhaps this is why it's tempting to stick a screen in front of them to keep them entertained or at least distract them from being sad.[8] But it's not working. The *World Happiness Report* shows that American young people are among the unhappiest in the world, and their growing unhappiness parallels that of the world's most war-torn, desperate nations.[9]

Ironically, seeking happiness isn't what makes you happy. Rather, happiness comes from successfully handling and recovering from struggles, difficulties, and disappointments. Children who learn to do this become resilient.[10] If they don't learn these skills, they'll be fragile and more vulnerable to cultural lies. For example, the first time they hear they must have been born in the wrong body they might agree because it helps explain their discomfort.

> Happiness comes from successfully handling and recovering from struggles, difficulties, and disappointments. Children who learn to do this become resilient.

Resilient children and parents know life won't always be easy. They don't panic when it's not. Instead, they embrace the purposeful tension that forces them to grow, and growing people are happier. You need this ability, and so do your children. Sometimes, our loving heavenly Father shapes us by allowing us to be challenged. It doesn't feel good, but in the end, we become more like Jesus.[11]

Preparing Boys and Girls and You to Stand for Truth—Three Tested Strategies

This is why it is essential to be strong and let our *yes* be *yes* and our *no* be *no*.[12] It's important not to let your children manipulate you. Don't let them convince you that you must make their path smooth. Don't let them avoid challenges or quit because it's hard. If you rescue them too soon, you'll steal their victory. Instead, cheer them to think and act upon what is right.[13] Going through challenges, not around them, is a surer path to life satisfaction.

> **If you rescue them too soon, you'll steal their victory.**

James 1:2–3 instructs us to count trials as joy, because they produce steadfastness. Social science research reveals the wisdom of this approach. Adam Alter, a best-selling author and professor at New York University, uses the term *hardship inoculation* to describe a skill that successful people cultivate. They don't flee hardship. They seek it, in small ways, every day. Those minor hardships build resilience.[14]

We're convinced that Gen Z's struggles with anxiety and depression are related to an inability to grapple with hardship. Young adults who believe God has given them what they need to rise above anxiety, and who act on this belief in the face of hardship, find significant relief from anxiety.

HOW TO SAY IT

- "I know this is hard. But hard is not bad. Hard is just hard and you've done other hard things. I want you to be the kind of person who feels pride at pushing through, accomplishes much, and becomes a better person. It's what God wants."

Be Prepared to Stand When Challenged

Conversations with people who've bought into transgenderism are hard because adherents believe themselves to be their own source of truth, unhooked from the real world.

RAISING GENDER-CONFIDENT KIDS

In this kind of situation, we prefer using questions to make people think. A good question keeps on asking long after the conversation is over. People may be unable or unwilling to answer the question when you ask it, but you'll get them thinking. Be prepared to continue the conversation when they're ready. Here are some illustrations:

- When someone announces that they are transgender, ask, "Would you be willing to share what happened to you that causes you to see yourself the way you do?"
- When someone calls you a hateful name for what you believe, say, "I see that you're angry, but is there a way we can talk about this without name calling?"
- When a child teases a child by saying, "You run like a girl. Are you sure you aren't a girl?", teach them to smile and say, "Nope, I'm a boy. That's just how I run."
- When an adult child accuses you of being hateful because you believe the Bible, say, "I love you and always will. But I am uncomfortable with violating my conscience as a condition of loving you. How can we move forward even though we disagree?"
- Gender ideology is obsessed with fitting everyone into a box. Innumerable online "quizzes" promise to help you determine which of 68 genders you are. You don't have to attack the idea. Just say, "Do you think that it is respectful to put everyone in a box based on the latest terminology people have made up?"
- When someone insists that how they feel about gender is what is true, you can ask, "Feelings are important, but are they the most important thing? I've felt worthless before, but it's not true that I am worthless just because I felt that way. How do we get our feelings to line up with what is true?"

Preparing Boys and Girls and You to Stand for Truth—Three Tested Strategies

Pray for Miracles

Children need to borrow your faith as they develop their own. Let your kids blame you when they're challenged. It's okay to be the bad guy. For example, when peers confront your children for not accepting transgender ideology, encourage them to say, "This is what my parents taught me. I know they love me and other things they've taught me are true and helpful. I'm not the kind of person to turn against them just because someone who doesn't even love me disagrees with what they believe."

But as children's faith grows, we also need to pray, in faith, for miracles in their lives. Mark 9:24 records a remarkable conversation between Jesus and a man desperate for his son to be healed of demon possession. When Jesus asked if he believed, the man replied, "I believe. Help my unbelief." What a remarkable prayer! We, too, need to pray to Jesus to give us faith that our children will love God and become gender confident.

We believe in miracles. In the summer Summit Ministries programs, students who are angry at God learn to love and trust him. Students are healed from addiction. Students whose eyes are blinded to the truth come to see it clearly. We see students set free from bad beliefs. Don't tell us that miracles don't happen. We see hundreds of them every year!

God loves working miracles in the lives of His children. And he loves it when we claim Jesus' resurrection power and believe that impossible situations can turn around. He loves it when we seek His kingdom and righteousness. Matthew 7:11 says, "If you then, who

> **God loves working miracles in the lives of His children.**

are evil, know how to give good gifts to your children, how much more will your Father who is in heaven give good things to those who ask him!"

Pray that children will take on God's perspective. "Father, I lift up this child to you in the name of Jesus, to see what you see, to hear what you hear, and to want to go where your attention is directed."

Here is a weekly prayer guide for miracles in the lives of the children you love:

Sunday. Pray that their minds will be sharpened. God wants us to love him with our minds. It is never God's will that we learn to obey so that we may think less. *"Father, in Jesus's name, I pray that this child will learn to value and discern truth (John 17:17), take every thought captive (2 Corinthians 10:5), not be taken captive (Colossians 2:8), and be the kind of person who helps others be set free" (2 Timothy 2:24–26).*

Monday. Pray that they will have hope. Hope is our deposit on the eternal destiny God has promised. Hope makes people resilient, builds mental health, promotes good deeds, and inspires positive emotions. *"Father, in the name of Jesus, I pray for the miracle of hope to fill my children's minds and souls. Give them the instinct to know how much they mean to you, to claim the living hope that you promise through the resurrection of Jesus (1 Peter 1:3) and to overflow with hope through your Holy Spirit" (Romans 15:13).*

Tuesday. Pray that they will acknowledge the Lordship of Jesus Christ. More than 700 times, the New Testament refers to Jesus as Lord. A "lord" is one who has complete authority. Jesus said that all authority in heaven and on earth has been given to him (Matthew 28:18). Jesus will "re" everything—renew, restore, redeem, and reconcile. *"Father, I pray this in the name of Jesus Christ the Lord, that my child will acknowledge Jesus as Lord of everything, every aspect of life, and experience the joy of being transformed in every way to be like the Lord Jesus."*

Wednesday. Pray for persistence in the face of trials. Because God has granted us eternal life, we can know that our momentary trials purify us like fine gold (1 Peter 1:7). *"Father, you say in your Word that our trials bring praise, honor, and glory to your son Jesus. I pray in His name that each trial* *my children face today will turn to gold. That they will be sure of your presence, confident in your love, and that they will be a blessing to everyone they meet."*

Thursday. Pray for hearts to be pure. Jesus said that the pure in heart will be blessed (Matthew 5:8). *"Lord Jesus, you said that the pure in heart will see God. I pray that my children's hearts will be pure and clean and clear of evil thoughts. I pray that their hearts will be joyful and hopeful, especially when things don't go their way."*

Friday. Pray that they'll love God more. Twice each day, our Jewish friends recite the Shema from Deuteronomy 6. "Hear, O Israel: The Lord our God, the Lord is one. You shall love the Lord your God with all your heart and with all your soul and with all your might." *"Loving Father, I pray that my children will love you with all their emotions, with everything that makes them alive, and with all of the strength I know you will give them to face whatever comes."*

Saturday. Pray that they'll be people of compassion and grace. *"Holy Spirit, will you guide my children today to grow in character by being kind to one another, to have tender hearts toward each other, to be quick to forgive because your Son has offered them forgiveness (Ephesians 4:32). I pray that they will remember that they are under grace, not law, and that they'll receive that grace when they make mistakes, or are unsure of themselves, or when they feel like condemning themselves (Romans 6:14). May they see themselves more clearly today as your beloved children"* (1 John 3:2).

OUR PRAYER FOR YOU BASED ON GOD'S PROMISES

We need God's truth so we can be clear about what God says, discern the lies the culture tells, treat others with dignity even when we think they are wrong, and be released from guilt and shame.

Now is the time to stand. The enemy is hard at work confusing children so that they lose trust in God. Learning to stand for truth the Jesus way takes time and practice. But we have the power of God's presence, through prayer and encouragement. We are never at a loss for something to do!

The God we serve is the Creator of the whole world and the Savior of our souls. He is still in the miracle business.

It's hard to know how to close a book like this, but we'd like to do so by offering a prayer for you. Will you take a moment to go to a quiet place in your heart and receive this prayer with faith?

> *"Loving heavenly Father, we come to you with freedom and confidence (Ephesians 3:12). You are our helper; we will not be afraid (Hebrews 13:6). You are our refuge and strength. Therefore, we will not fear even though the earth trembles and the mountains tumble into the sea (Psalm 46:1–3). We pause and contemplate this with every fiber of our being. We pray for parents and children who grow to be humble and wise (Romans 5:3–4, James 4:10, 1 Peter 5:6, Proverbs 9:10). We pray for quiet confidence in you, and a radiant spirit that brings peace and hope. We picture our children as boys who mature into godly men and girls into godly women. We envision this not to meet our own expectations, but because of who you have lovingly designed them to be. May they not have a spirit of fear, but one of power, love, and self-control (2 Timothy 1:7). And we pray that, as you encouraged Joshua and so many others, we will be strong and of good courage all our days (Joshua 1:9). We pray that the same power that raised Jesus from the dead would be in us, and in our children (Romans 8:11). Make us a blessing to all nations of the earth (Galatians 3:8). Amen."*

DR. JEFF'S PERSPECTIVE
THE POWER OF PRAYER

When one of my sons was a little boy, he was plagued by bad dreams. I asked him, "Would you like me to pray for you?"

He nodded and closed his eyes.

I prayed, "God, help my son have good dreams tonight, dreams about puppies and kittens and birds."

His eyes flew open. "Birds aren't nice," he said accusingly.

I was struck when I realized I wasn't really praying in faith. I was just trying to "psych" my son into not having bad dreams.

"I'm really sorry, son," I said. "Can I start over?"

He nodded and closed his eyes again.

I prayed, "God, I pray that *this very night* you will raise up my son to be a man of courage. I pray that when hard things come, he will know your presence. I pray that when enemies come, he will stand strong. I pray that he will be the kind of man who stands up for those who are weak and protects them."

The terrifying dreams stopped. Throughout his school years, my son was known as the boy who would stand up for the "little guy." Now, he's preparing to become a firefighter.

Our prayers with and for our children speak prophetically over them, orienting their thinking toward God and unleashing their calling.

DR. KATHY'S PERSPECTIVE
TEACH CHILDREN TO PRAY FOR THEMSELVES

When my nieces and nephew were young and I visited, I enjoyed watching and listening to their bedtime routine with my brother and sister-in-law.

Among other things, each child reached into a jar to pull out a name of someone to pray for—teachers, missionaries, neighbors, friends, family members, and of course, their beloved dog, Snickers. But do you know whose names weren't in the jars? Theirs.

Dave, Debbie, and I talked about the value of Betsy, Katie, and Andy learning to pray for themselves and the needs they were aware of. There will be times when children may not have someone present to pray for them. Or they may be uncomfortable being vulnerable even with you and may not verbalize a prayer request. Children need to know they can talk directly to God in prayer! When children pray for themselves aloud, you will learn what is important to them. Is it happiness, a better relationship with their youth pastor, a good piano lesson with their teacher, or do you hear their hearts pray for a friend who's scared that her parents may get a divorce? Now you can affirm them, offer input if they want you to (but don't take God's place!), follow through, and help them discern God's answers.

> Want this prayer guide pinned to the family bulletin board, in your purse, or tucked in your Bible? Download the "Weekly Prayer Guide" at genderconfidentkids.com.

STRAIGHTFORWARD ANSWERS TO OUR 24 MOST FREQUENTLY ASKED QUESTIONS

1. **How do I help my child feel confident in their God-given gender?**

    Confidence comes from two words, *together* and *faith*. A confident child gathers strength from trusted individuals to believe what is true and live in a new way. So, be confident and trustworthy—and it's okay if you don't know everything. Admitting when you don't (yet) can increase children's trust in you. Express compassion for their struggles, communicate hope that this struggle will end and they will be stronger for it, and teach them to see and apply the truth of God's Word. The truth we want them to understand is that God intentionally made them the way he did on purpose, and it is beautiful.

Be available and love your children unconditionally so they listen to you and are influenced by you. Many others want to tell them how to live or influence them toward what is false. These people don't know or love your children. God knows and loves them and will give them the strength to believe they are *not* mistakes. Open the Word with them and let them hear you pray for them, including for courage to believe that they don't need to reinvent themselves to fit in or feel safe, popular, or beautiful. Their body isn't broken. Who they are—male or female—is part of their purpose, not something they need to figure out or fight for. You could also consider reading sections of this book to them.

2. How can I model gender confidence as a parent?

As we've seen throughout this book, wise parents work to keep the lines of communication open by listening well, teaching God's truth in a helpful way, and asking meaningful questions so you're a source of security. Act on and talk about truths in the chapters about God's design for boys and girls. Be honest about your childhood struggles. Most children find it hard to believe that their parents, who seem decisive and strong, ever faced struggles. Say, "As I was growing up, I remember feeling out of place and wondering whether God really made me on purpose. It took me a long time, but I learned to trust God that he was working everything out for my good. Trusting him and changing some of my attitudes was necessary. I'm grateful and I believe this will happen for you, too."

Straightforward Answers to our 24 Most Frequently Asked Questions

3. **It seems like gender confidence is related to overall confidence in life. How can I help my child be secure in who God made them to be?**

   You're right. Identity confidence gives rise to gender confidence. In Kathy's book, *Five to Thrive*, she shows how children have core needs for security, identity, belonging, purpose, and competence. We encourage you to refer to Chapter Three, where we share these in detail. Usually, when a child seems to be losing confidence, one or more needs strengthening. Remember that the order of the needs is significant. Therefore, you can strengthen a need by addressing it *and* the ones below and above it. Children will embrace more of life when they know and love God, trust Christ, believe that God has thoughtfully and wonderfully made them, including for a relationship with Himself, that life is an exciting exploration about the passions God has given us though which we can glorify him, and that we've been designed to have a positive influence on those around us. Talk about and model these truths.

4. **At what age should I start talking to my child about gender?**

   How you talk about gender identity depends on what children are experiencing and their age and maturity level. You can use direct instruction, read and discuss biblically accurate children's books, and use teachable moments.

   It is usually appropriate to talk with elementary-age children about how God made boys and girls differently and wants them to grow up to be men and women who love him and serve others.

For middle school children, it is important to tie discussions about gender identity into what you share about puberty. Explain that part of becoming a man or woman is going through physical changes. These changes are natural but may seem awkward to themselves and their peers. Middle school may be a good time to talk about what we've shared about becoming confident men and women.

For most high-school-age children, identity questions shift from gender to wondering about what they're good at and what they might want to do with their lives. Jeff's book *Truth Changes Everything* shares about men and women whose belief in Jesus turned them into difference-makers in everything from medicine to education to science. This helps them see how God uses what they do to make a living to change the world for the better. This is also a good time to emphasize the different kinds of smarts we've included in the book, especially in the chapter about raising girls. (Kathy's book, *8 Great Smarts*, will help you identify your children's strengths and how to use them.) Also, pray for discernment so you'll discover what your children do to energize themselves, increase their joy, and help them accomplish good work. Help them learn how they work best with others.

At all ages, it's important to emphasize that God has made us purposefully and wants us to trust him and stand for what is true even when it's hard.

5. What words or phrases should I avoid when discussing gender?

It is essential to avoid language that makes gender seem like a spectrum, with extreme femininity on one end and extreme masculinity on the other. We don't want girls thinking their gender is a mistake if their behavior appears to be more similar to the boys they know than the girls they know, on a scale like this. The same is true for boys. Boys and girls each have their own spectrum of traits and interests, which is part of God's design. Some boys are aggressive, others are quieter and thoughtful. Some girls are more tomboyish, others are drawn toward very feminine things. And many are both! Kathy danced when she was young, loved the frilly costumes, got dirty and sweaty playing softball, and did well in honors math and science classes. Jeff didn't enjoy organized sports but loved competing in speech and debate. He didn't enjoy math, but did enjoy playing the piano and singing. It's important to root discussions of gender in God's design, not stereotypes or "how we feel today."

6. How can I explain gender confusion to my child without introducing ideas they're not ready for?

We can imagine a conversation about gender going like this: "At some point, everybody feels out of sorts, as if they don't quite fit in the world. Some people get so confused that they think they may have even been born in the wrong body. Some girls think they are stuck in a boy's body. Some boys think they are stuck in a girl's body. Sometimes they try to comfort themselves by dressing up to look the way they think boys or girls look. It's very sad and difficult and we need to be kind to them. But God makes everyone the way he wants them to be. He doesn't make mistakes. He created you, loves you, and knows what's best for you. He knows that sometimes you feel uncomfortable growing up, like you don't fit in with others. That happened to me for a while. But the one thing you can be sure of is that God made boys and girls on purpose so they can work together to stand for what is right and be a blessing to others."

7. **What do terms like *gender dysphoria, non-binary,* and others related to this topic mean? How should I explain them to my children?**

   Older children may wonder about these terms, having heard them at school or in conversations with their peers. If so, you can explain them this way:

   "It's sad to think about, but a lot of people are disappointed in one or more parts of their lives. They feel sad for no reason, try to figure out why, and want the disappointment and sadness to go away. Gender dysphoria means people are very stressed about being born a boy or girl. They don't just not like it; they *really* don't like it. They think about being born in the wrong body all the time and think if they change their body, they'll be happy. This happens to very few people, but unfortunately a lot of people talk about it on the internet and on television and make people who aren't comfortable with all parts of their bodies wonder whether they may have gender dysphoria. Some of these people call themselves non-binary, which means that they don't think of themselves as a boy or a girl. This is very sad, too, because God designed boys and girls on purpose. Maybe they're confused because they were bullied, something went wrong in their family, or they haven't learned to trust that God knew what he was doing when he made them. We want to be kind to people who are having a hard time, just as we would be kind to someone who uses a wheelchair and has a hard time getting around, or someone who is teased to the point where it makes them sad or mad. I want you to know that God made you the way he did on purpose. He loves you and loves that you're a boy or girl. Because he loves us, he wants us to grow strong through the challenges we face, so we live in a way that makes people want to know God and love him. Always make sure to let me know if you have other questions about this or about how you feel."

Straightforward Answers to our 24 Most Frequently Asked Questions

8. How do other biological or developmental issues (hormonal imbalances, diet issues, neurodivergence, etc.) affect my child's gender and identity formation?

There does not appear to be a relationship between hormonal imbalances and transgenderism. The relationship between diet and transgenderism is two-fold. People who gravitate toward transgenderism, as we've noted, nearly always experience comorbidities such as anxiety and depression. Eating disorders such as overeating or restrictive eating are related to these comorbidities. Also, medical intervention such as hormone therapy can have negative side effects of weight gain (along with other serious side effects, such as cardiovascular disease, diabetes, and osteoporosis). Research has credibly shown a link between transgenderism and autism. In some studies, transgender-identifying people were up to six times as likely as non-transgender-identifying people to report autism traits.[1]

No one knows exactly why, but it could be that individuals on the autism spectrum may latch on to the current popularity of transgenderism as a means of winning the social approval that they otherwise find difficult to obtain. It's important to know that not all children on the spectrum will struggle with this.

9. What should I say if my child says they feel like the opposite gender?

We respect that this can be a scary conversation. Not expressing shock or anger is vital because you want your child to keep talking. Kathy recommends that parents practice using their "stone face" at times like this. Thank them for confiding in you about something so difficult. Start by asking them to elaborate. You might find out they were teased, so they're questioning their gender, but don't *feel* like the opposite gender. Or maybe they read something on the internet and now assume they may have been born in the wrong body. The source of their confusion will direct your conversation. Be encouraged that nearly all children identify with their God-given gender by the time they reach the end of their teen years if there's no social or medical transitioning.[2]

During this time, it is vital to reinforce relationships with their same-gender parent and/or godly individuals of the same gender, remove negative influences as much as possible, and promote opportunities to form positive peer relationships. Also, cultivate conversation about all kinds of things the child enjoys rather than frequently focusing on gender discomfort. Throughout, the message is, "God created you the way he did on purpose. He thought you through and made you just the way he wants you to be, and it is good. Sometimes we don't feel that the way we were made is right. You're not crazy and you're not alone. We're going to focus on finding areas where you can excel and be a blessing to others. We're going to believe you'll be open to God changing your attitudes and beliefs to align with his."

10. How can we love and support kids who are struggling with gender identity without affirming gender ideology?

It is never appropriate to tease or shun a person who is gender insecure. But it is also important not to be unduly influenced by them. While their transgender appearance is the most obvious thing about them, based on the way they look, dress, or act, transgender-identifying people are like all other people. They have hopes, dreams, and interests. They have other concerns and struggles. Find common ground on what you can. Talk about those things while you agree to disagree regarding whether changing gender is possible or good. Part of growing up in a diverse culture is learning to have compassion toward people without forfeiting your beliefs, caring for them without making them an object of pity or obsession, and respecting and standing up for your beliefs without quarreling.

11. What are some ways to reinforce gender identity through everyday life (not always making it "a thing")?

As children grow, they learn to change their focus and priorities by noticing what and how other people do things, how they feel, and how they can learn from their positive or negative examples to do what is right. Children pay attention to what you praise, so notice what others do well and talk about it. Mention it when you see boys and girls, and men and women, acting in a godly way based on their gender, but don't talk about it all the time. Create moments when children can see that your gender serves you well. Talk about positive opportunities that both genders have in your community. With your own children, reinforce the good God is doing in their lives by saying, "You were careful/diligent/wise with that," or "I noticed you were very focused and energized when you worked on 'X'. I think that tells us something about how God made you," or "The most important thing you can do in the world is love God and love others. Let's talk about how we can both do this even better."

12. How do I create an open space for questions without compromise?

Remember and reread our suggestions at the end of Chapter Four about using questions well. Talking with someone is an act of intimacy because you're communicating mind-to-mind and heart-to-heart. It can be natural to begin to see the world from their viewpoint or at least understand why they see things as they do. Those who aren't firm in their biblical worldview might say, "They're a person too. And the more I talk to them, the more I think that they're just fine the way they are. *I'm* the one who needs to change." This person may say to others, "If you knew them the way I know them, you wouldn't think they're so wrong." But a more biblical response is, "I accept that this person is, like all people, a person with dignity as an image-bearer of God. But, like all people, they can be misled, and they have a sin nature. My goal for them is the same as the goal for myself, to be transformed by the power of Christ and to become more like Jesus. I withhold my opinion about what I think about them—how nice they are, how reasonable they seem—and seek to see them from the perspective of God who wants them to be healthy, whole, and in a relationship with Jesus."

13. What are some biblical ways to teach true masculinity and femininity for kids growing up in today's culture?

Show your son that you see him becoming a man—applying the five core needs and strengthening weaker ones will help. Affirm his attributes and character qualities and how God might use them; don't assume he'll know. Teach him about leadership. If he's insecure about his physical strength or prowess, talk with him to put it in perspective and do anything else that would help. Help him identify wise men he would like to know or have as role models because of their careers, healthy marriages, role as dads, or talents. Help him arrange to meet them. Explore possible jobs that fit his interests, gifts, and passions. Help him see that real men work to improve themselves, are servants who pay attention to what is needed, and choose to help others. Help him become a warrior for truth who stands for what is right and becomes increasingly bold and skilled at standing against what is wrong. Praise him when he does good work and help him see that godly men are hard workers whose work makes a difference to those around them.

Show your daughter that you see her becoming a woman and use the five core needs to convince her. Pay attention to her so she knows you're safe to process doubts and delights with. Take insecurities about her physical appearance seriously, help her put them into perspective, and help her make appropriate changes if she wants to. Affirm her personality, character qualities, and other attributes and how God might use them; don't assume she'll know. Ensure she doesn't see her sensitive and gentle side as a weakness. Teach her about following and submitting well, and that she can also appropriately lead. Help her identify wise women she would like to know or have as role models because of their healthy marriages, roles as moms, contentment as single women, or success in their vocations. Celebrate her desire to be married and be a mom; this is something almost no one in today's culture will do for her. Communicate clearly with grace, patience, and kindness. Help her discern truth, stand up for it, and teach it to others.

14. How can single parents reinforce gender confidence without a second role model (therefore lacking the opposite gender) at home?

Bonding with the same-gender parent is part of bringing a young adult back into congruence with their natal sex, along with counseling (with a Christian counselor), adjustments of life habits, elimination of the transgender influence (for example, social media), and separating the child from negative peer group influences. The same-gender role model can be a grandparent, uncle, aunt, coach, teacher, youth group leader, or another willing adult. Spending time with families that have stable marriages and strong parent–child relationships will also be helpful. If you're a single parent because of divorce, avoid speaking condemningly about your ex-spouse. Over time, this diminishes your child's respect for you and may lead them to draw incorrect conclusions about their gender based on the negativity of that relationship.

15. How can I use social media positively to reinforce my child's gender confidence?

Kathy's book, *Screens and Teens,* is a helpful resource to guide your children through their use of technology. Although social media platforms change, they are probably here to stay. Even if you limit their use, your children will be around peers who use them. Social media amplifies, rather than changes, people. Those with a spirit of anger use it to vent. Those who feel insecure use it to get people to feel sorry for them. Those who seek popularity use it to "edit" their lives to appear something more than what they are. So, it's essential to teach children how to think about what people post and why. Ask questions like, "What do you think that person wants to communicate to others?", "How should we treat them?", and "What are some things we tend to place our identity in, rather than Jesus?" And teach them to think about what they post and why. Are they motivated by insecurities, jealousy, revenge, or a need to compare? To use social media to positively reinforce gender confidence, they can post truth, debunk stereotypes, follow positive influences, and block negative ones. And always realize that if social media takes children away from genuine relationships in the real world, then it is doing more harm than good.

16. How can I protect my children from confusing online content? How can I know if they are being affected by it?

Keeping devices out of children's bedrooms is always smart, and being available so they can tell you what they've seen or read is wise. Be sad before getting mad, or they may stop coming to you. Focus on seeing things biblically so they learn to compare what they read or hear to God's Word. Teach them to discern so they know the difference between what is good and evil, real or fake, and prefer what is good and real.[3] As a parent, you'll know they're being negatively affected by online content because there will be an emotional barrier between the two of you and they may ignore you and be rebellious. Also, you'll hear them talk about and agree with ideas you haven't taught them that contradict their upbringing.

17. What do I do if my child's school pushes non-biblical gender ideology?

When voices shout that "gender is a spectrum" or "You can be whoever you feel like today," kids without a biblical worldview may quickly lose sight of what's true. Even those with biblical beliefs can be persuaded to shift beliefs if the manipulators are especially powerful. If this happens in your child's school, and school officials lie about what they're doing or try to hide it from parents, it's probably time to seriously consider leaving. We say this recognizing that such a change is difficult. But once evil has taken root, it won't be uprooted without a fight. If a school is willing to indoctrinate children with lies about gender identity, what other false ideologies will they also promote? Your primary responsibility is to *your* children. In many communities, there are Christian schools that honor God and see their primary mission as helping parents disciple their children.

Homeschooling is also a great option. It's mainstream now, with excellent resources and support, and groups of parents cooperating to help their children obtain an excellent education. We work with children from all sorts of backgrounds, and in our experience, children who have been homeschooled for at least some of their lives are among the most secure, curious, and resilient.

If you decide to stay and fight, which you need to know in advance will be like nailing Jell-O to the wall, we recommend banding together with other parents with similar concerns. Share this book with them. Recognize that while many (perhaps most) teachers genuinely want to help children, an increasing number have chosen to be educators because they fervently want to impose wrong worldviews on children. If the school is deeply committed to so-called gender affirming care, ask to see the resources and evidence. Approach the situation with grace, but firmness: "I appreciate your wanting to avoid bullying and help children feel safe, but the best available evidence is that making a big deal out of gender identity is confusing to children who don't struggle and provides worse outcomes over time. And it's unfair to overload teachers with tasks they don't want and force them to implement an agenda based on untested theories, and that causes them to lose credibility with children and parents."

18. How do I prepare my teen for potential workplace challenges related to biblical beliefs about gender?

It's a virtual certainty that your child will face transgender ideology in the workplace. It may be mandated by the employer to use preferred pronouns, affirm transgender, participate in diversity training designed to promote transgenderism, and work with transgender colleagues. It is important to keep the lines of communication open

Straightforward Answers to our 24 Most Frequently Asked Questions

about what their work colleagues discuss and believe. Emphasize that it is never appropriate to make fun of gender insecure colleagues or agree with those who do.

If your son or daughter is forced to submit as a condition of employment, encourage them to say, "I work hard to make our company successful, and I respect the dignity of my colleagues. But my conscience tells me this is not the best way." Your conscience is one of your most important gifts. It is something you must live with your whole life.

If their colleagues become angry with this stance, encourage your child not to take it personally. People who are "sexual minorities" may demand affirmation to the point of projecting onto others the shame they feel at their own confusion. When they say, "Shame on you," it's not a statement about you. It's a statement about themselves. Believers don't operate on a shame culture, but on a dignity culture. We don't *give* people dignity; we *recognize* their dignity as image-bearers of God, no matter how broken. If your child loses the job, encourage them to rely on God to protect and care for them. He promises he will. In Matthew 6:31–33, Jesus says, "Therefore do not be anxious, saying, 'What shall we eat?' or 'What shall we drink?' or 'What shall we wear?' For the Gentiles seek after all these things, and your heavenly Father knows that you need them all. But seek first the kingdom of God and his righteousness, and all these things will be added to you."

19. How do I respond to family members or friends who disagree with our beliefs?

Most families manage to relate to one another just fine despite divergent beliefs. If you're asked, use this book as a reference to explain the positive case for what you believe and why: "I know that many people struggle with many things and use different sources of truth. In our family we believe what the Bible teaches, and we're focused on helping meet our children's core needs and being confident in who God made them to be." If this leads to a debate, remember three things. First, acknowledge the differences. "We have differences and that's okay." Second, focus on commonalities. "We both care about making life better for those around us." Third, be friendly, but don't grovel or compromise. "I know we don't see eye-to-eye, but you've given me a lot to think about and I hope you feel the same."

20. How do I teach my child to love peers with different beliefs without compromising our faith?

We know this isn't just a question because of gender ideology. We imagine you deal with this for several false beliefs. Learning to love peers with different beliefs starts when children are very young and disagree over the simplest things: "Mommy, Angela's favorite color is yellow! That's not a good color!" How you encourage children to handle simple things like this will come back to bless them when life gets more complex. Teach that we can disagree and still love people. Teach about love from 1 Corinthians 13:4–8 and explain the need to stand from 2 Timothy 2:24–26, "The Lord's servant must not quarrel, but must be gentle to everyone, able to teach, and patient, instructing his opponents with gentleness. Perhaps God will grant them repentance, leading them to a knowledge of the truth. Then they may escape the trap of the devil who has taken them captive to do his will."

Straightforward Answers to our 24 Most Frequently Asked Questions

21. Should I let my children hang out with transgender-identifying peers?

In decades of working with young adults, we've learned that children will not go further in life than the companions they choose. Who you hang out with will influence you. We are to be friendly to all, but the friends we choose should be people who lift us up and challenge us to be all we are designed to be. Pray for such friends for your children. Make your home a place where such friendships can be nurtured. One problem that many young adults have with their friend group, especially girls, is that when one child is especially wounded and especially vocal, it can cause peers to take on their negativity and woundedness. Psychologists call this co-rumination. Whether your child can handle such relationships without succumbing to wrong perspectives on life is a difficult judgment that must be made with prayer and discernment. It should be based on 2 Timothy 2, which says that we are to be gentle to others, seeking to persuade them in the hope that they may be set free from the devil's snare. Boundaries are crucial if no such opportunity exists or if the friend is resistant to truth.

22. How much should I engage with people who embrace transgender ideology?

Students at Summit Ministries have told us that when they try to engage gender insecure people, it just makes everyone mad. So, when should you engage? A good rule of thumb is to ask, "Is there anything I can say that could cause you to see this issue, or me, differently?" If the answer is "No," the person's *arguments* are probably not worth engaging with. But don't give up *on the person*. People miraculously change all the time by God's grace. Your approach is that of a missionary. You want everyone not to be deluded, to turn toward God, and to come to the knowledge of the truth about Jesus.

23. What should I say if my child's friend asks them to use different pronouns?

Insisting on personal pronouns is one of the most significant aspects of the transgender agenda. In most cases, in English, you don't need pronouns to talk *to* a person, but only when talking to others *about* them. If the topic arises, though, we need to learn to say, "I want you to know that I respect you and I will call you by whatever name you prefer. But my conscience tells me that pronouns are statements about reality, not preferences. So, I hope you'll respect my conscience as I respect yours."

Please understand that there is a debate about this in the Christian community. Some advocate what they call "pronoun hospitality," which is using each person's selected pronouns to show graciousness. But shouldn't it be possible to be hospitable while being honest? A name is a referent. People pick names and nicknames all the time. But pronouns are a statement about reality. We hate to think that the use of pronouns would turn someone against God, but we also need to remember that what you attract them *with* is what you attract them *to*. If transgender-identifying people realize later that the Bible doesn't support transgenderism's core assumptions, they'll feel tricked. In church, we need to be able to say, "None of us are here just to feel affirmed. Often, we feel convicted. The goal of this church isn't to help us speak our own truth, but to help us seek *the* truth. Every week we must recognize that we aren't the center of reality at all. Jesus is. And he wants us to be healthy and whole so we can help others flourish."

24. Isn't your focus on gender just a political talking point rather than a real issue?

Many think that our focus on gender ideology is somehow political, that we're picking on people who are different. They say, "Why can't you just leave them alone?" But our focus is on helping our children be confident in their gender and inoculated against messages that confuse them and cause them to doubt the goodness of their created design. Unfortunately, it is the case that people in the transgender community and those who support them believe that it helps struggling people to punish those who disagree with transgender ideology or are reluctant to submit to the insistence on using preferred pronouns. Debating about such things makes people angry. But there is no reason a progressive must cease being a progressive to say, "We shouldn't be telling kids they can be born in the wrong bodies."

For more FAQs, updated regularly, download the "Ever-growing FAQs" at genderconfidentkids.com.

ACKNOWLEDGEMENTS

Dr. Jeff Myers:

I would like to thank Dr. Kathy for making this project so meaningful and fun. You've shown the power of iron sharpening iron through encouragement, questions, discussion, and a cheerfully relentless pursuit of excellence. I'm grateful for the Summit Ministries students I've worked with over the years, for the laughter and tears, for the honesty about their challenges, and for their openness to being transformed by the power of Christ. What hope for the future! The Summit Ministries publishing team is remarkable. They love Jesus, they work quickly and accurately, and make writing fun. Director of Publishing Aaron Klemm, your vision for how Summit Ministries can minister to this generation of parents is the "behind the scenes" inspiration for this project; you're making a once-in-a-generation difference. Thank you also to Dr. Carol Allston-Stiles and Dr. Trent Langhofer for your helpful input. Finally, I'd like to thank the financial partners who have jump-started Summit Publishing and the media team at EPIC for their enthusiasm in spreading the word.

Acknowledgements

Dr. Kathy Koch:

Thank you, Dr. Jeff, for wanting to partner with me. I had a lot of passion for a book like this, but passion isn't enough. My dream only became a reality when you invited me to write with you. I needed your expertise and the support of your publishing team. It's always been a privilege to partner with Summit Ministries as a member of your faculty, and now this! Thank you for your trust, openness, commitment to truth, and respect for my ideas. I'm also grateful for youth, parents, and educators who shared concerns and stories with me through the years and who told me to write this book. I'm grateful for everyone at Summit, and especially Aaron Klemm, who welcomed me as one of Summit's own and never made me feel like an outsider who was in the way. I couldn't have written this book without the guidance and support of Wayne Stender, the Celebrate Kids COO. Thank you for talking through some of this content with me, gently suggesting and holding me to deadlines, taking on many responsibilities, and willingly writing Chapter Seven, with the help of your wife, Nancy. I'm so glad she's on our team, too! I'm also grateful for our prayer warriors and contributors who God uses to extend our ministry.

ABOUT THE AUTHORS

DR. KATHY KOCH

Dr. Kathy Koch ("cook") is the founder and president of Celebrate Kids, Inc. A former university professor turned child celebration advocate, she desires for everyone she encounters to know they are created on purpose, with purpose, for a purpose.

Dr. Kathy earned her PhD in reading and educational psychology from Purdue University. Her faith in God, classroom experience, and years of study have shaped best-selling books like *8 Great Smarts*, *Screens and Teens*, and *Five to Thrive*—resources now used in homes, schools, churches, and universities.

Kathy's workshops include practical insights, object lessons, and strategies that turn theory into action. Her audiences always walk away with data, an understanding of culture, clear frameworks, and examples from real-life stories.

Most of all, Dr. Kathy values people. Whether praying with a grandparent, greeting a shy kindergartner, coaching weary moms at conventions

About the Authors

and church gatherings, or even when on a stage, Dr. Kathy aims for connection. She believes that people learn, heal, and flourish when they feel seen and valued.

Dr. Kathy loves offering clear steps, solid reasoning, creative sparks, and heartfelt encouragement. Connect with Kathy at her next speaking event, in her next book, or by tuning into a podcast at celebratekids.com.

CELEBRATE KIDS

Celebrate Kids, Inc., exists to instill confidence, curiosity, character, and Christ-centered purpose in every child. By speaking to every smart, core need, and major question kids have, they develop an identity in Christ and purpose for God. Founded by Dr. Kathy Koch in 1991, Celebrate Kids delivers research-based, biblically-solid keynote addresses, seminars, podcasts, and books used in 30 countries.

Partnering with schools, churches, organizations, and families to nurture academic growth and spiritual health, Celebrate Kids' programs rest on three pillars—security, identity, and belonging. Through the study of Scripture, culture, people, and child development, Celebrate Kids offers frameworks through books like *8 Great Smarts* and *Five to Thrive*, arming adults with clear models that result in measurable outcomes.

Every seminar, online course, and podcast from Celebrate Kids connects concepts to concrete care with stories. Parents, educators, counselors, pastors, and leaders benefit from Celebrate Kids' resources with practical activities, explanations of child and teen development, cultural analysis, conversation scripts, and questions that spark dinner-table connections. Celebrate Kids equips the adults who shape kids, so children hear—loud and clear—"God made you smart on purpose, with purpose, for a purpose."

DR. JEFF

Dr. Jeff Myers has served as president of Summit Ministries since 2011. His introduction to Summit Ministries was as high school graduate skeptical about Christianity. Through Summit Ministries, Dr. Jeff dug in and studied a biblical worldview, ultimately trusting Jesus Christ as his Lord and Savior.

Dr. Jeff's life mission is to prepare a rising generation of godly leaders. With his background as a high school and college debating champion and debate coach, he's passionate about helping young leaders overcome fear to communicate with clarity and grace. After earning a Doctor of Philosophy degree with a focus on human communication studies from the University of Denver, Dr. Jeff served as a professor at Bryan College, where he taught undergraduate and MBA students. As an entrepreneur, Dr. Jeff founded several businesses related to leadership and communication training.

Dr. Jeff has authored 19 books and has become one of America's most respected authorities on youth leadership development. Focus on the Family founder Dr. James Dobson referred to him as "a very gifted and inspirational leader." Evangelist Josh McDowell called him "a man who is 100% sold out to preparing the next generation to reflect the character of Christ in the culture."

Dr. Jeff's worldview trilogy—*Understanding the Faith*, *Understanding the Times*, and *Understanding the Culture*—have become the standard texts for training high school students in a biblical worldview. His book *Exposing the Gender Lie*, co-authored with Brandon Showalter, helped spark state and federal policy changes toward transgender ideology.

Dr. Jeff's speaking schedule includes churches, homeschool conferences, policy events, businesses, colleges, banquets, and workshops focused on leadership and a biblical worldview. His media appearances and weekly Truth Changes Everything podcast articulate a biblical worldview and annually help millions of people gain confidence in biblical truth.

About the Authors

SUMMIT MINISTRIES

Summit Ministries equips and supports the rising generation to embrace God's truth and champion a biblical worldview. Started in 1962 by Dr. David and Alice Noebel, Summit Ministries introduced the idea of "worldview" to America's youth. Through its conferences, curricula, and dozens of spin-off ministries, Summit Ministries has mobilized four generations of believers to transform a broken world through a biblical worldview.

Summit Ministries' broad offerings include summer intensives for 16–22-year-olds, biblical worldview and apologetics curricula for Christian schools, homeschools, churches, and public school release time programs, mass-market publishing of timely resources applying a biblical worldview to seemingly impossible issues, training for Christian teachers, customized worldview training events, and media and social media commentary.

NOTES

Preface

[1] Proverbs 25:11.

[2] Forces in our culture seek to distinguish *sex* and *gender*, claiming that *sex* refers to physiological attributes and *gender* refers to the mental perception of sexual identity. This distinction is nearly always treated as a fact, when in reality it is a twisting of language foisted on people by transgender activists. In this book, as we mentioned in the text, we had to decide whether to use *gender*—which has become political, or *sex*—which nearly always refers to sexual activity, not sexual phenotypes. We've chosen to use the word *gender*. Our thinking is based on the root word of gender, the word *genus* which means birth, family, or nation. It refers to the first thing we know about a creature after its basic creaturely attributes are identified. For example, the cat *genus* includes different kinds of cats. But from Genesis 1:27, which we take to be inspired Scripture, the first thing we know about humans is that God created them male and female. This was said of no other creature in the creation account. The maleness and femaleness of humans is the most important thing God wants us to know about them, next to the fact that they are human. Other creatures were listed according to their "kind." Humans are not. So, the *genus* of humanity is male and female. It isn't just a sexual phenotype. You may not agree with how we're approaching this, but at least you know where we're coming from, and it hopefully won't be a stumbling block as we explore how to help boys become godly young men and girls become godly young women.

[3] Moran Gershoni and Shmuel Pietrokovski. "The landscape of sex-differential transcriptome and its consequent selection in human adults," BMC Biology 15, no. 7 (2017), DOI: 10.1186/s12915-017-0352-z.

Notes

Chapter One

[1] Anna Brown, "About 5% of young adults in the U.S. say their gender is different from their sex assigned at birth," Pew Research Center, June 7, 2022. https://www.pewresearch.org/short-reads/2022/06/07/about-5-of-young-adults-in-the-u-s-say-their-gender-is-different-from-their-sex-assigned-at-birth/.

[2] See Exodus 20:12; Deuteronomy 6:6–9; Proverbs 1:8, 6:20–22; Ephesians 6:1-4; Colossians 3:20.

[3] Hebrews 10:23

[4] Psalm 7:5.

[5] Genesis 1:27.

[6] John 10:10.

Chapter Two

[1] Romans 12:2, Ephesians 4:22–24.

[2] Ephesians 6:10–18.

[3] "52% of teens are 'very motivated' to learn about Jesus," Barna Research Group, January 30, 2025. https://www.barna.com/trends/teens-curious-about-jesus/.

[4] Romans 12:2 and Ephesians 4:22–24.

[5] Romans 10:9.

[6] Moran Gershoni and Shmuel Pietrokovski, "The landscape of sex-differential transcriptome and its consequent selection in human adults," *BMC Biology* 15, no. 7 (2017), https://doi.org/10.1186/s12915-017-0352-z.

[7] Lisa Littman, "Parent reports of adolescents and young adults perceived to show signs of a rapid onset of gender dysphoria," *PLOS One*, August 16, 2018, https://journals.plos.org/plosone/article?id=10.1371/journal.pone.0202330.

[8] "Gender Dysphoria Diagnosis," *American Psychiatric Association*, https://www.psychiatry.org/psychiatrists/diversity/education/transgender-and-gender-nonconforming-patients/gender-dysphoria-diagnosis.

[9] María Paz-Otero, Antonio Becerra-Fernández, Gilberto Pérez-López, and Domingo Ly-Pen, A 2020 Review of Mental Health Comorbidity in Gender Dysphoric and Gender Non-Conforming People, *Journal of Psychiatry Treatment and Research* 3, no. 1, March 6, 2021. https://scholars.direct/Articles/psychiatry/jptr-3-007.php?jid=psychiatry.

[10] Other examples you may be familiar with include that a woman is a "person with a cervix," pregnant women are "pregnant people," and breastfeeding moms are "chest feeders."

[11] Implemented specific inclusive practices in sexual health education, *Lead Health Education Teacher Surveys*, 2022, *Centers for Disease Control and Prevention*, https://profiles-explorer.cdc.gov/#/table/?questionId=SN24&LocationAbbr=ALL&subQuestionId=T_Q14_1&year=2022.

The page includes the following notes: "Per a court order, HHS is required to restore this website as of 11:59PM ET, February 14, 2025. Any information on this page promoting gender ideology is extremely inaccurate and disconnected from the immutable biological reality that there are two sexes, male and female. The Trump Administration rejects gender ideology and condemns the harms it causes to children, by promoting their chemical and surgical mutilation, and to women, by depriving them of their dignity, safety, well-being, and opportunities. This page does not reflect biological reality and therefore the Administration and this Department rejects it." Accessed May 9, 2025.

[12] Kyle Lukoff, *When Aidan Became a Brother* (New York: Lee & Low Books, 2019); DeShanna Neal and Trinity Neal, *My Rainbow* (New York: Kokila/Penguin Random House, 2020); Leslea Newman and Maria Mola, *Sparkle Boy* (New York: Lee & Low Books, 2017).

[13] Luona Lin, Juliana Menasce Horowitz, Kiley Hurstand, and Dana Braga, Race and LGBTQ Issues in K-12 Schools, *Pew Research Center*, February 22, 2024. https://www.pewresearch.org/social-trends/2024/02/22/race-and-lgbtq-issues-in-k-12-schools/.

[14] "Poll: Majority of Parents Oppose Transgender Ideology in Schools," *Decision Magazine*, January 13, 2025. https://decisionmagazine.com/poll-majority-of-parents-oppose-transgender-ideology-in-schools/.

[15] We respect Laura Perry Smalt's testimony and recommend her book *Transgender to Transformed: A Story of Transition That Will Truly Set You Free* (Bartlesville, OK: Genesis Publishing Group, 2019). See also "From Transgender to Transformed With Laura Perry Smalts," Strong Women Podcast, May 28, 2024, https://colsoncenter.org/strong-women/from-transgender-to-transformed-with-laura-perry-smalts, and "Laura Perry Smalts' Authentic Shift From Transgenderism to Embracing God's Design," *Focus on the Family*, https://www.focusonthefamily.com/parenting/transformed-by-faith-laura-perry-smalts-journey-from-transgenderism-to-embracing-gods-design/.

[16] Josie A. and Dina S., *Parents with Inconvenient Truths about Trans: Tales from the Home Front in the Fight to Save Our Kids* (Pitchstone Publishing, 2023), p. 335, and Clinical Advisory Network on Sex and Gender, "Summary of Cass Review," Clinical Advisory Network on Sex and Gender, April 28, 2024, https://can-sg.org/2024/04/28/summary-of-cass-review/.

[17] See Jeff Myers and Brandon Showalter, *Exposing the Gender Lie: How to Protect Children and Teen from the Transgender Industry's False Ideology* (Manitou Springs, CO: Summit Ministries, 2022). https://www.summit.org/resources/articles/exposing-the-gender-lie-the-reason-for-concern/.

[18] See Jennifer Bilek, "Big Pharma, Big Tech, and Synthetic Sex Identities," (lecture, Hillsdale College Kirby Center, Washington, D.C., July 28, 2022), https://freedomlibrary.hillsdale.edu/programs/campus-lectures/big-pharma-big-tech-and-synthetic-sex-identities, and Sue Donym (pseudonym), "The New Conversion Therapy: How Homophobic Quackery is Targeting Children," December 2022, https://archive.ph/kJ2Gg.

Notes

[19] "The Cass Report Is Out—An Early Analysis of Findings and Recommendations," *Do No Harm*, April 11, 2024, https://donoharmmedicine.org/2024/04/11/cass-report-slams-gender-affirming-care-model/.

[20] The following executive orders are catalogued at the Federal Register: The Daily Journal of the Federal Government, https://www.federalregister.gov/; Executive Order 14168 of January 20, 2025: Defending Women From Gender Ideology Extremism and Restoring Biological Truth to the Federal Government, https://www.federalregister.gov/documents/2025/01/30/2025-02090/defending-women-from-gender-ideology-extremism-and-restoring-biological-truth-to-the-federal; Executive Order 14187 of January 28, 2025: Protecting Children From Chemical and Surgical Mutilation, https://www.federalregister.gov/documents/2025/02/03/2025-02194/protecting-children-from-chemical-and-surgical-mutilation; Executive Order 14190 of January 29, 2025: Ending Radical Indoctrination in K-12 Schooling, https://www.federalregister.gov/documents/2025/02/03/2025-02232/ending-radical-indoctrination-in-k-12-schooling; and Executive Order 14201 of February 5, 2025: Keeping Men Out of Women's Sports, https://www.federalregister.gov/documents/2025/02/11/2025-02513/keeping-men-out-of-womens-sports.

[21] NCAA Media Center, "NCAA announces transgender student-athlete participation policy change," February 6, 2025, https://www.ncaa.org/news/2025/2/6/media-center-ncaa-announces-transgender-student-athlete-participation-policy-change.aspx.

[22] Christopher Schorr, "State Reforms to Protect Children from Harmful and Irreversible Transgender Medical Procedures," *America First Policy Institute*, March 12, 2025, https://americafirstpolicy.com/issues/state-reforms-to-protect-children-from-harmful-and-irreversible-transgender-medical-procedures.

Chapter Three

[1] Kathy's book about the core needs is *Five to Thrive: How to Determine if Your Core Needs Are Being Met (and What to Do When They're Not.* (Chicago, IL: Moody Publishers, 2020). Because of the relevance and importance of the core needs, she also includes them in each of her other books.

[2] John 3:16, Genesis 1:27, Jeremiah 31:3.

[3] Romans 6:11, John 8:32, Romans 12:2, Romans 8:37.

[4] Ephesians 1:7, Ephesians 2:10, Colossians 2:10, Romans 8:1, 2 Corinthians 5:21, Galatians 5:22.

[5] Ephesians 1:6, Psalm 27:10, 2 Corinthians 1:4, John 15:15, Ephesians 1:5, Isaiah 43:1.

[6] Matthew 22:36–40.

[7] Matthew 28:18–20.

[8] Ephesians 6:10, Philippians 4:8–9, Philippians 3:14, Ephesians 2:10, 1 Corinthians 6:11.

[9] Philippians 4:13, 1 Corinthians 2:16, 2 Corinthians 10:5, 1 Corinthians 6:19, 2 Corinthians 12:9, Hebrews 13:6.

Chapter Four

[1] Summit Ministries has published several excellent resources about biblical worldview formation. We encourage you to check out the blogs, newsletters, and podcasts of Dr. Roger Erdvig and Dr. Maggie Pope at Summit Ministries, https://www.summit.org/educators/center-for-biblical-worldview-formation/. If you want to go in-depth, consider: Roger Erdvig, *Beyond Biblical Integration: Immersing You and Your Students in a Biblical Worldview* (Manitou Springs, CO: Summit Ministries, 2020).

[2] Jeremiah 17:9.

[3] Natasha Crain, *Talking with Your Kids About God: 30 Conversations Every Christian Parent Must Have* (Ada, MI: Baker Books, 2017).

[4] See mamabearapologetics.com and Hillary Morgan Ferrer (ed.), *Mama Bear Apologetics: Empowering Your Kids to Challenge Cultural Lies* (Eugene, OR: Harvest House, 2019).

[5] Hebrews 4:12.

[6] John 8:32.

[7] Kathy Koch, *8 Great Smarts: Discover and Nurture Your Child's Intelligences* (Chicago: Moody Publishers, 2016).

Chapter Five

[1] Genesis 1:26.

[2] "Forging Godly Men in a Culture of Compromise," *Truth Changes Everything Podcast*, February 18, 2025.

[3] Romans 12:2.

[4] See Jonathan Burnside, *God, Justice, and Society: Aspects of Law and Legality in the Bible* (New York: Oxford University Press, 2010).

[5] Dennis Prager, *The Rational Bible: Numbers: God and Man in the Wilderness* (New York: Regnery Faith, 2024), 243.

[6] "Hesuchia," *Strong's Bible Dictionary 2271, BibleHub*, https://biblehub.com/greek/2271.htm. Accessed April 23, 2025.

[7] We recognize that people debate about the "complementarian" versus "egalitarian" interpretation of Paul's writings. While this might be top of mind for some readers, none of the parents or students whose counsel we sought on this book mentioned it as an overriding concern. That's why we're staying focused on raising boys and girls who are confident in God's design for their gender.

[8] Jeff Myers and Brandon Showalter, *Exposing the Gender Lie: How to Protect Children and Teens from the Transgender Industry's False Ideology* (Manitou Springs, CO: Summit Ministries, 2023).

[9] No civilization has attempted to remove the stabilizing influence of man/woman marriage and survived. For more detail on the centrality of man/woman marriage, see chapter 10, Jeff Myers, *Understanding the Culture: A Survey of Cultural Engagement* (Colorado Springs: David C. Cook, 2017).

Notes

[10] *Economics* is based on two Greek words, *oikos* meaning *household* and *nomos* meaning *rule*. Economics literally means the rule of a household. Households, not businesses, are the basic unit of analysis in economics. Even today, 90 percent of businesses are family enterprises.

[11] The Buddha said, "Of all the scents that can enslave, none is more lethal than that of a woman. Of all the tastes that can enslave, no is more lethal than that of a woman. Of all the voices that can enslave, none is more lethal than that of a woman. Of all the caresses that can enslave, none is more lethal than that of a woman."

[12] Brandon Showalter, "Artificial Intelligence, Transhumanism and the Church: How Should Christians Respond?" *The Christian Post online*, January 27, 2018, https://www.christianpost.com/news/artificial-intelligence-transhumanism-and-the-church-how-should-christians-respond.html.

[13] 1 Corinthians 6:19–20.

[14] Moran Gershoni and Shmuel Pietrokovski, "The Landscape of Sex-differential Transcriptome and its Consequent Selection in Human Adults" *BMC Biology* 15, no. 7 (2017), https://doi.org/10.1186/s12915-017-0352-zDOI: 10.1186/s12915-017-0352-z.

[15] Quoted in Leonard Sax, *Girls on the Edge: The Four Factors Driving the New Crisis for Girls—Sexual Identity, the Cyberbubble, Obsessions, Environmental Toxins* (New York: Basic Books, 2020), 86.

[16] Colossians 3:2.

[17] Galatians 5:13.

[18] Mark 10:45.

[19] 1 Corinthians 11:1.

[20] Candace West and Don H. Zimmerman, "Doing Gender," *Gender and Society* 1, no. 2 (June 1987), 125, https://www.jstor.org/stable/189945.

Chapter Six

[1] "Data and Statistics on ADHD," *Centers for Disease Control*, November 19, 2024, https://www.cdc.gov/adhd/data/index.html.

[2] Mary Elizabeth Williams, "Patriarchy harms boys and men, too. Helping them realize this is the key to erasing toxic masculinity," *Salon*, June 8, 2024, https://www.salon.com/2024/06/08/patriarchy-harms-boys-and-men-too-helping-them-realize-this-is-key-to-erasing-masculinity/.

[3] Christina Hoff Sommers, *The War Against Boys: How Misguided Feminism is Harming Our Young Men* (New York: Simon and Schuster, 2000), 13.

[4] Harvey C. Mansfield, *Manliness* (New Haven, CT: Yale University Press), 229.

[5] Dan Hart, "Young People Are Driving Increase in Faith, Church Attendance in West, Reports Say," *The Washington Stand*, April 11, 2025, https://washingtonstand.com/news/young-people-are-driving-increase-in-faith-church-attendance-in-west-reports-say-.

[6] Jeff Myers, "The New Rise of Men: Why Gen Z Males Voted for Trump," *Washington Times*, November 15, 2024, https://www.washingtontimes.com/news/2024/nov/15/gen-z-males-voted-trump/.

[7] See Nancy Pearcey, *The Toxic War on Masculinity: How Christianity Reconciles the Sexes* (Grand Rapids, MI: Baker Books, 2023).

[8] Rhonda Stoppe, *Moms Raising Sons to be Men* (Eugene, OR: Harvest House, 2023), 122.

[9] Jim Elliot, *The Journals of Jim Elliot* (Grand Rapids, MI: Fleming H. Revell, 1983), 174.

[10] "Inmate Sex," *Federal Bureau of Prisons*, April 26, 2025, https://www.bop.gov/about/statistics/statistics_inmate_gender.jsp. Accessed May 1, 2025.

[11] Michael Kimmel, "Almost all violent extremists share one thing: their gender," *The Guardian*, April 8, 2018, https://www.theguardian.com/world/2018/apr/08/violent-extremists-share-one-thing-gender-michael-kimmel.

[12] See Mark Roseman, *The Villa, the Lake, the Meeting: Wannsee and the Final Solution* (London: Allen Lane/Penguin, 2002).

[13] Girls are more likely to process stimuli through the prefrontal cortex (by thinking) and boys in the amygdala (by acting). See Leonard Sax, *Why Gender Matters: What Parents and Teachers Need to Know about the Emerging Science of Sex Differences* (New York: Broadway Books, 2005), 14, 18, 30.

[14] See 1 Kings 12.

[15] J. C. Ryle, "Dangers of Young Men," section 2, part 5: "Another Danger to Young Men is the Fear of Man's Opinion." *Thoughts for Young Men*, in the public domain, 17. Free online at https://www.preachtheword.com/bookstore/thoughts.pdf.

[16] Jordan B. Peterson, @jordanbpeterson, "People grow up when they get married. It is probably better to get married when you are young because then you grow up. And then what else matures people? I have met very few people who have fully matured . . . ," *X*, July 24, 2024, 10:38 am, https://x.com/jordanbpeterson/status/1817238065275961480.

[17] Thank you to Scott Turansky and Joann Miller for this excellent definition of honor, from their book *Say Goodbye to Whining, Complaining, and Bad Attitudes: In You and In Your Kids* (New York: PRH Christian Publishing, 2000), 13.

[18] See Luke 15:11–32.

[19] Malory Locklear, "Brave or reckless? Thrill-seekers' brains can tell you," *New Scientist*, October 9, 2014, https://www.newscientist.com/article/dn26353-brave-or-reckless-thrill-seekers-brains-can-tell-you/#:~:text=The%20brave%20feel%20fear%20but,military%2C%20says%20Mujica%2DParodi.

[20] Ana Sandoui, "Why men might find multitasking more challenging," *Medical News Today*, November 20, 2016, https://www.medicalnewstoday.com/articles/314219#Studying-task-switching-in-men-and-women.

Chapter Seven

[1] Kathy Koch, *8 Great Smarts: Discover and Nurture Your Child's Intelligences.* (Chicago, IL: Moody Publishers, 2016), https://celebratekids.com/8greatsmarts.

Notes

[2] Howard Gardner, "Multiple Intelligences: New Horizons in Theory and Practice" and Thomas Armstrong, "Multiple Intelligences in the Classroom."
[3] Koch, *8 Great Smarts*.
[4] Proverbs 1:20–33.
[5] Acts 16:14–15.
[6] Exodus 31.
[7] Acts 9.
[8] Exodus 15:20–21.
[9] Psalm 33:9.
[10] Genesis 21:8–21.
[11] Genesis 29.
[12] Genesis 2:4–3:24.
[13] Esther 5:1–6:11.
[14] Acts 18:18–28.
[15] Luke 15.
[16] 1 Samuel 1:1–2:10.
[17] Luke 2:19.
[18] Luke 5:1–15.
[19] Matthew 9:4–38.
[20] John 17.

Chapter Eight

[1] Alycia Wood, "Understanding Gender, Intersex, and Sexuality," The Truth Changes Everything Podcast, September 10, 2024, https://www.summit.org/resources/podcast/understanding-gender-intersex-sexuality-alycia-wood/.
[2] Leonard Sax, *Why Gender Matters: What Parents and Teachers Need to Know about the Emerging Science of Sex Differences* (New York: Broadway Books, 2005), 237.
[3] Sax, *Why Gender Matters*, 35.
[4] As of this writing, a debate is raging between different types of feminists. Some, such as Christina Hoff Sommers, believe that males and females have different "essences" that are more than just clumsy attempts to force boys and girls into blue and pink cubbyholes. But others openly advocate things like boys competing in girls' sports, even though it seems self-defeating. Why? Modern feminism insists that no meaningful difference exists between males and females, not because the evidence points that way, but because they're concerned that if differences between males and females turn out to be real, it will reinforce "toxic" masculinity, diminish the claims of LGBTQ people, and result in discrimination. To this way of thinking, the question, "What is a woman?" is illegitimate because to base the answer in biology—that a woman is an adult human female—will ultimately hurt the cause of women. See, for example, Suzanna Weiss,

"Why I Can't Get on Board with 'Embracing Differences Between Men and Women' for Feminism," *Everyday Feminism*, January 15, 2017, https://everydayfeminism.com/2017/01/say-no-to-gender-essentialist-feminism/.

5 Sax, *Why Gender Matters*, 19.

6 Michael Peterson, "What Men and Women Value at Work: Implications for Workplace Health," *Gender Medicine* 1, no. 2 (December 2004): 106–24, https://doi.org/10.1016/S1550-8579(04)80016-0.

7 When females experience stress, norepinephrine is upregulated, which increases alertness, attention, and memory. When males experience stress, dopamine is upregulated, increasing motivation, energy, and aggression. The female effects are not seen in males, or vice versa. See Andre L Curtis, Thelma Bethea, and Rita J Valentino, "Sexually Dimorphic Responses of the Brain Norepinephrine System to Stress and Corticotropin-Releasing Factor," *Neuropsychopharmacology*, 31, 544–554, August 24, 2005, https://www.nature.com/articles/1300875.

8 Sax, *Why Gender Matters*, 14, 18, 30.

9 Michael Gurian, *The Purpose of Boys: Helping Our Sons Find Meaning, Significance, and Direction in Their Lives* (Hoboken, NJ: Jossey-Bass, 2010), 34.

Chapter Nine

1 Michael Gryboski, "Leaving Christianity: What are the statistical trends?", *Christian Post*, October 27, 2019, https://www.christianpost.com/news/leaving-christianity-what-are-the-statistical-trends.html?page=2.

2 Kerith J. Conron, Shoshana K. Goldberg, and Kathryn O'Neill, "Religiosity among LGBT adults in the US," Williams Institute, October 2020, https://williamsinstitute.law.ucla.edu/wp-content/uploads/LGBT-Religiosity-Oct-2020.pdf.

3 See "PRRI Generation Z Fact Sheet," Public Religion Research Institute, March 29, 2024, https://www.prri.org/spotlight/prri-generation-z-fact-sheet/; Samantha Kamman, "Only a quarter of Gen Z attends church at least once a month, survey finds," *Christian Post*, February 13, 2023, https://www.christianpost.com/news/only-28-of-gen-z-attends-church-at-least-once-a-month-survey.html.

4 Kendall Qualls, "Hope for American Families," *The Truth Changes Everything Podcast*, September 10, 2024, https://www.summit.org/resources/podcast/the-prodigal-project-hope-for-american-families-kendall-qualls/.

5 Dennis Prager, *The Rational Bible: Numbers—God and Man in the Wilderness* (New York: Regnery Faith, 2024), 4.

6 Hebrews 13:5.

7 Deuteronomy 31:8.

8 "I need to be happy all the time" is one of the lies technology causes children to believe that Kathy teaches in her book: Kathy Koch, *Screens and Teens: Connecting with Our Kids in a Wireless World*. (Chicago, IL: Moody Publishers, 2015).

9 In the 2024 *World Happiness Report*, figure 2.5 lists nations listed by the changes in

Notes

happiness from 2006–2010 to 2021–2023. The United States is listed at 120 and Congo (Kinshasa) listed at 123, meaning that they are among the nations that have had the greatest net negative changes of the 134 nations listed. See John F. Helliwell, Richard Layard, Jeffrey D. Sachs, Jan-Emmanuel De Neve, Lara B. Aknin, and Shun Wang (eds), *World Happiness Report*, University of Oxford: Wellbeing Research Centre, 2024, 38. https://worldhappiness.report/ed/2024/.

[10] Kathy wrote an entire book about resilience and Jeff wrote the foreword because we both believe in its value for parents and children. Kathy Koch, *Resilient Kids: Raising Them to Embrace Life with Confidence*. (Chicago, IL: Moody Publishers, 2022).

[11] Romans 8:29.

[12] Matthew 5:37.

[13] Philippians 4:8.

[14] See Adam Alter, *Anatomy of a Breakthrough: How to Get Unstuck When It Matters Most* (New York: Simon and Schuster, 2023).

FAQ

[1] Varun Warrier, et al., "Elevated rates of autism, other neurodevelopmental and psychiatric diagnoses, and autistic traits in transgender and gender-diverse individuals," *Nature Communications* 11, 3959 (2020), https://doi.org/10.1038/s41467-020-17794-1.

[2] Miriam Grossman, *Lost in Trans Nation: A Child Psychiatrist's Guide out of the Madness* (New York: Simon and Schuster, 2023), 38.

[3] Our favorite definition of discernment comes from an editorial comment by Charles Grosvenor Osgood, who edited *Boswell's Life of Johnson*. It is as follows: "But the supreme end of education, we are told, is expert discernment in all things—the power to tell the good from the bad, the genuine from the counterfeit, and to prefer the good and the genuine to the bad and the counterfeit." Charles Grosvenor Osgood Editor's note by Charles Grosvenor Osgood (ed.), quoted in James Boswell, *Boswell's Life of Johnson* (New York: Charles Scribner and Sons, 1917), xviii.

How Jesus Followers of the Past Teach Us to Live Boldly Today

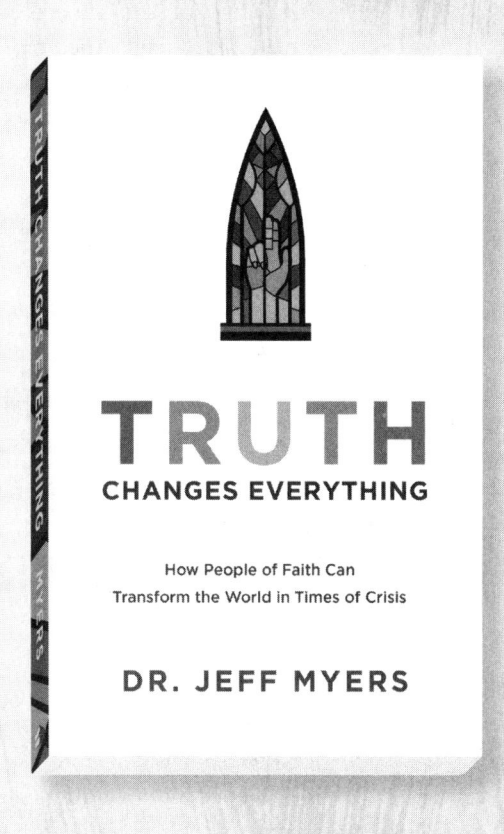

TRUTH CHANGES EVERYTHING

How People of Faith Can Transform the World in Times of Crisis

DR. JEFF MYERS

Dr. Jeff Myers vividly illustrates how ordinary people who believed in Truth—not the relative "truths" of our current postmodern and pluralistic culture—transformed society in times of crisis, and how you can do the same today.

Visit summit.org/tce to learn more and purchase.

Resilient Kids equips adults to nurture children's God-given capacity to bounce back from adversity. Kathy Koch spotlights thirteen "resilience robbers" such as entitlement and screen dependence, then replaces them with gratitude, responsibility, and service. Practical guidance shows how meeting five core needs cultivates courageous learners who adapt, persevere, and thrive.

Five to Thrive reveals five core needs—security, identity, belonging, purpose, competence—that shape self-worth. Kathy Koch helps adults discern when needs are unmet and meet them biblically through words, discipline, and technology choices. Stories, inventories, and action steps empower families, classrooms, and churches to raise motivated, resilient children and renewed adults.

8 Great Smarts celebrates every child's intelligence by expanding Gardner's theory through a biblical lens. Kathy Koch describes word, logic, picture, music, body, nature, people, and self smarts, offering inventories, activities, and discipline tips. Parents learn to recognize strengths, develop weaker areas, and encourage children to glorify God with gifts.

Get these books, online courses, and more at celebratekids.com.